# Raising **Boys** Who **Become** Remarkable **Men**

*Kathryne Savage Imabayashi*

# Dedication

*This book is dedicated to three of the most important men in my world.*

Firstly, to my brother John, whose feedback, suggestions, and edits have profoundly shaped this book. I'm grateful for his generous support and the time he dedicated to helping me.

To my husband, Hiromi, who unconditionally supports me each and every step of this mission, always giving me encouragement and belief in myself whenever I start to waver. Thank you for the emotional support that helped me to keep going.

Lastly, to the man who set it all in motion, Toshi. This book would not exist without your entrance into our world. Your belief in your mom, your support when I struggled, and your timely advice form the backbone of this book. Toshi, you continue to inspire me to never give up on a dream, and I take such pride in the beautiful man you've become. Thank you for being our remarkable man!

I also want to thank two wonderful women, Vicky Enea & Amy Spencer, whose feedback at the end of this process helped me to be able to push that button to get this out into the world.

# About the *Author*

*Kathryne Savage Imabayashi*
*Founder of Sonhood Coaching*

Born into a family of eight, all female except for two, Kathy grew up as a member of the baby boomer generation. She envisioned and created a series of life's adventures often based on intuition, or more often, on a feeling inspired from a book.

Little did she know that reading *Shogun* by James Clavell would propel her into an international journey and nomad lifestyle that would start in Japan and take her through six very distinct countries and cultures.

Kathy had a rich and diverse career in education for more than four decades. Her heart is with the youngest of children and most of her teaching years were within the area of Early Years Education. Kathy also possesses expertise in guiding and nurturing children throughout their elementary years. She taught in both national and international schools, founded her own preschool in Japan and for the last decade of her career worked leading teachers and supporting families in school leadership roles. Whether in the role of teacher, coordinator, vice principal or principal, for every decision ever made, and continues to make, the guiding influence is always, 'Is this in the best interest of the child?'

That mantra directed Kathy, with the birth of their son, to understand more deeply about the inner emotional world of boys and begin a movement to challenge how our society is doing a dis-service to our boys in particular, but to all males. Today she continues to advocate for all boys and support their parents and teachers to help raise these boys to become remarkable men. Kathy works with families and schools sharing her knowledge and giving strategies that will create an environment where our boys are better understood and respected for their own uniqueness.

## Table of Contents

# *Prologue*

When I am searching for answers in life, I always turn to books. Somehow, the right book appears at just the moment I really need it. I approach an author's credibility with scrutiny. Are they genuinely well informed and trustworthy, or are they simply a skilled wordsmith trying to make a living?

When seeking advice on dog training, it's improbable that I'd choose a book written by someone who hasn't personally owned a dog. Authentic expertise in canine matters arises from a deep bond with a canine companion. This bond reflects a genuine affection for your dog, where its well-being significantly impacts your daily life. You consistently safeguard it from potential harm and strive to enhance its life. It's only when a dog holds a substantial place in your life and heart that your authority truly resonates with me.

My bio informs you that I have the experience and education to wield authority. And while that is important, it's my role as a mother to a boy that has inspired a resource that will change how you parent your son and how you relate to all the males in your world.

Before my son was born I had been working with young children for almost two decades. I understood these precious little humans and I was dedicated to creating the best educational experience for them. I had confidence in my ability to impact children's lives, and their parents.

The missing piece was that I had no idea of what I didn't know about being a parent. I didn't understand that overpowering feeling of protection that seemed to accompany my baby even before he entered the outside world. I lacked a frame of reference for that all-encompassing and unconditional love that moved me to tears as I considered the future moment when he would venture beyond the security of our home and confront a tougher world, a thought that played on my heart even while we were still in the hospital!

I had not yet experienced the confusion of why my son was treated differently than my friend's daughter. I didn't yet know the frustration I would feel when other boys would hurt him and they were not held accountable. I hadn't yet felt the loneliness of feeling like I was the only parent trying to raise my boy differently. And I hadn't yet been ostracized and harshly judged for choosing to remove my son from an environment that did not keep him safe.

I also hadn't experienced the sense of awe when watching this beautiful boy demonstrate how wonderful the world is through curious and innocent eyes. I didn't know that the moment I reconnected with him at the end of my day, I would start to breathe deeper and feel that now my world was complete. I hadn't understood the pure joy of being woken up with a set of small arms wrapping themselves around my neck, and feeling that I was the most important person in the world to another human being.

I know these things now. That is why I wrote this book for you. For him.

I have traveled the road and my son has become a remarkable man. For three decades he has been the source of inspiration and strength that turned challenging times into bearable ones and elevated ordinary times into something extraordinary.

I have learned more from him than any other person or book I have encountered – and I've come across a multitude of both. Through him, I've gained insights into myself, my partner, and of course, my son. These insights extend to boys in general and their relationship with parents.

I am now acutely aware that as parents, our influence is profound, surpassing our comprehension. We possess an incredible opportunity, accompanied by a weighty responsibility to profoundly impact our boys' perspectives on the world and how they live in it.

This book has the power to bring about positive change, and the world of our boys will be enriched from you having read it. That is my motivation for creating it and why I believe I am a credible authority worth considering.

*A young mother looks down at her newborn son and thinks:*

How can I make sure that he is going to turn out OK?

How can I protect him from succumbing to what others think he should be?

What will happen when he starts venturing out in the world and is baffled and frustrated with how he is being treated, because he is a boy?

Is he going to be safe when he walks down the street as a teenage boy?

Will he look for an escape with some external crutch? Drugs? Alcohol?

How can I be certain that he won't turn out like some of the toxic males we read about?

How am I supposed to raise this innocent, precious boy when I don't really understand his inner, emotional world?

# *Why did I write this book?*

Occasionally I've wondered how our son's life might have unfolded had we not been so intentional in our parenting.

Would we have had more turbulent times because we simply weren't aware of all the factors influencing his inner emotional world?

Would he have felt the need to wear more and more masks in order to simply survive in his world? Would we have lost the real little boy I knew he was?

It paints a pretty bleak picture and my heart breaks to imagine it.

This book is written to help parents give their sons the best fighting chance possible.

Our son has grown into a wonderful adult, a remarkable man.

We have had our share of challenges that come with parenting, and he needed to pass through the tough times that most boys experience growing up.

I have had my share of sleepless nights worrying about our parenting and praying we were doing the best for our son.

I worked hard to understand how to do this, and need to share this with you.

Today I have a son that I not only love beyond comprehension, but who I really like as a person.

He is kind and caring, combining the best of both parents and infusing that with his own identity. He has become a strong, independent man who makes an impact on those in his world.

We have long, interesting conversations where he freely shares his perspectives and can also really listen to mine.

Some of our roles have flipped as the years have passed, and now he gives me advice, support and counsel in areas I am weak in - like technology!

He also holds me accountable, especially connected with my mission to help other boys and their parents in today's world.

My hope is for parents to experience the joy that is in my parenting world today. It hasn't always been easy and it is far from perfect. There was a time when I really feared we might lose him down a path that could only end up badly. I believe his upbringing and his understanding that his parents loved him unconditionally helped him pass through those rebellious years. We got through them, together. We have a profound connection that allows for rich and deep communication, and the love is strong. Parenting is a lot of work. It is hard sometimes. But there is nothing so important and nothing so beautiful as seeing your son be the person he can be.

Parenting a son in today's world presents unique challenges. Approximately 5% to 10% of children in their early years of formal education are diagnosed with ADHD, a condition that is three times more prevalent in boys than girls. Boys naturally tend to be active and require movement, yet many classrooms do not adequately cater to this need. While some boys (and girls) benefit greatly from a diagnosis and subsequent support, I question whether a deeper understanding of the needs and learning styles of boys could lead to the creation of more inclusive environments that make a significant difference for our boys.

This current generation of parents is facing the challenge of addressing their sons' increasing desire to spend time on screens. Regulations are still being developed and research is not yet clear as to how much is too much, or how screen time is affecting our children. Understanding what goes on in the emotional world of boys can help parents set limits and boundaries that may be healthier for their child's development and growth.

As parents, you hold a significant amount of power and influence in your son's life. The challenges are real, whether age-old ones or ones still in the process of being defined, but it is so important that you recognize that you have the ability to make a difference.

You can do this through becoming aware of the challenges in your boy's world, then learning all that you can about gender differences, and finally jumping on that bandwagon and becoming your boy's greatest advocate. *This book is a great start!*

## *I grew up during the Women's Liberation Movement.*

I was part of the generation that coined the term 'male chauvinist pigs', referring to men who believed they were the superior race.

I was nurtured as a young girl, with the empowering notion that with hard work and determination, there were no doors I couldn't open simply because of my gender. I was as powerful as any male counterpart.

Women started to come into their own power. Helen Reddy's song, *I Am Woman,* symbolized the sentiment of the 70's. Women should no longer be submissive or accept an inferior social status. "I am strong. I am invincible. I am woman."

As a young woman I read self-help books like *The Cinderella Complex: Women's Hidden Fear of Independence,* and *The Peter Pan Syndrome: Men Who Have Never Grown Up.* As I bolstered my self-esteem and confidence, I also diminished and attempted to squash or counter male positions of authority.

I adopted the popular slogan that anything a man could do, a woman could do better. I was an independent career woman who did not 'need' a man in my life.

And then I gave birth to a male! How was I going to reckon with that? He certainly would not be one of those Peter Pan men. But how was I going to guide him to become a remarkable man?

## *When it all changed for me*

There was a critical turning point for me when my son was three.

After this incident my view about society's role in shaping how women relate to the male species altered drastically. And I slowly entered the inner world of what it really means to be a male.

*It was a Saturday.*
*My son and I went fishing along a serene*
*river, just down a quiet, country lane.*
*The sun was shining in a picturesque blue*
*sky and*
*a warm breeze rustled the branches of the*
*trees arching down the pathway.*
*It was a perfect day for a mom and her*
*son.*

*After we had been there for a while, I*
*looked up to see 'a gang of five or six boys'*
*making their way towards us.*
*My heart stopped.*
*Something so guttural and instinctive*
*spread panic through me. 'Oh my god - a*
*gang is coming and they probably will hurt us*
*both. What am I going to do to protect us?'*

*It turned out this 'gang' was a group of*
*upper elementary boys, the same age group I*
*was teaching at the time.*
*I should have known better than to react*
*solely on their size and their gender.*
*We were in no danger at all.*
*Quite the contrary.*

My reaction disturbed me greatly.

I later reflected on my instinctive reaction in the moment and attempted to understand the logic, or lack of it, behind the intensity of the experience.

But then came an image that became the catalyst for my future direction.

My heart broke to think that someone, someday, might see MY boy walk down a path, or down a street, or in the park and that fear would be the feeling that overwhelmed them.

**My boy?**
**Incomprehensible.**
**Utterly bizarre!**
**And solely because he is a boy?**

That image of some stranger being fearful of my little guy, my compassionate and empathic child, motivated me to action.

I began a crusade to learn and then teach why this societal reaction, my reaction, was outdated and unacceptable.

I started to learn everything I could about boys' development and those widely-held expectations that provide fertile ground for assumptions and prejudices.

And once I was on the path of educating myself, I became committed to also educating others. It became my mission!

Truly, there is nothing more powerful than a mission grounded in passion and purpose.

Then add that it is a mother's mission - well, mountains will be moved!

**That incident changed my world.**

Because of that fateful incident, I needed to re-evaluate my own responsibility in the current challenges associated with masculinity.

How much did women contribute to this world that has such archaic demands on our boys to behave and feel in certain ways?

To what extent are we, as parents, unconsciously influenced by gender biases, and how does this impact our perpetuation of stereotypical gender roles on our sons?

If I was a key player in the problem, did that mean I could also be a key player in finding a solution?

I had to examine deeply rooted and often unconscious ways I related to males, simply because they were males.

Did I assume most men fell into the categories of being potentially dangerous and sexual predators?

Did I assume they couldn't really be trusted?

Did I believe deep down they were not as powerful as women in any regard other than physical strength?

Was I numbly watching media that portrayed men as objects, as not as intelligent as most women, and as hard headed, macho guys?

Were they the butt of a lot of jokes in my favorite TV dramas?

Were the messages in those songs I sing along to talking about those men who still behave like boys? Or about the women who sing about their strength and power over men?

I had to discover all the things I didn't know about being male if I was going to do the best I could to raise my son.

I had to find out what the real differences were between men and women and how to work with those.

I needed to understand the challenges my boy was going to face in society, and then try and find tools that would help him stay true to himself, even when the pressure to be something else was great.

It felt overwhelming, a daunting task ahead of me. I wasn't sure I had the energy to pursue such a demanding undertaking.

And then I thought of why there really was no choice. My little boy. And all the little boys in the world. They deserved a chance to be understood.

They needed to feel the hope, the power, and the optimism for their future that I felt as a young girl.

Things have changed. Male chauvinist pigs have been renamed. Today we have a new term, 'toxic male', to describe exaggerated stereotype masculine traits that are widely accepted or glorified. Being 'a man' means you are physically strong, you are cool and don't show any weak or vulnerable emotions, you can take care of yourself and don't need anyone else, you always try to be #1, and you are the guy with all the sexual conquests notched on your belt.

This is part of the Boy Code mentality. Unlocking and unpacking this can be a great starting point in figuring out how to best parent your son.

Moms are usually their son's first love, first caregiver. He is connected to her in every way possible. All the messages she shares about males, consciously and not so consciously, either with her words or her actions, are going to set the groundwork for how this little guy relates to the world and sees himself in it.

If Mom tells him that boys don't cry, he will believe her, even when he doesn't understand why, and often feels he needs to cry. He will learn to hide that vulnerable part of himself so as to protect himself from shame and ridicule.

If Mom minimizes misbehavior with the thinking that accompanies, 'boys will be boys', he will learn that as he is a male, he will not be held accountable for some behaviour, and will be expected to act within acceptable male parameters. We normalize misbehavior by saying, 'it's a boy thing', and don't get too upset when they get into fights at school, or miss their weekend curfew.

If Mom shows disgust when he behaves in a way that is perceived weak or clingy, he learns to hide those feelings and incorporate what is acceptable. He loses his true self. He comes to understand she will not tolerate him being clingy nor protect and understand him when he is picked on or bullied by other boys.

Moms hold incredible power, especially during the first part of a little boy's life.

The more aware she is, the more knowledgeable she is, and the more she advocates for her boy, the better chance her son will have to face the challenges society is going to lay on him.

With her having his back he has a fighting chance!

Before long, your little boy is looking to his father to understand what it means to be male. He starts to want to mimic things his dad does like shaving, driving a car, carrying a briefcase as he goes to his pretend job.

He recognizes some similarities and begins to connect deeper. He begins to assimilate how his father shows up as a male; how he treats women; how he communicates; how he behaves; how he shows his feelings - or doesn't.

If he falls and hurts himself while out learning how to ride his bike with Dad, and is told to pick himself up - that boys don't cry; this little boy is going to deeply absorb that message.

If his dad says boys don't cry, and his dad never cries, then he may internalize the belief that if he shows any signs of crying, it means there is a serious issue or weakness within him.

If at the dinner table, his parents argue and his father belittles and shames his mother, your son may assume this is how men treat women.

If his mom cowers as his dad shouts out his anger, he will see this as an acceptable way to show your emotions. Being a man means it's ok to bully someone you are angry with.

Our actions are so powerful. Our children are always watching us.

But we also have the power to positively impact our sons.

We can completely rescript their experience.

Through our understanding and awareness, our boys can grow up knowing that the Boy Code exists, but with the inner strength to stay true to their authentic selves.

# *The Code*

*I don't care if it's a boy or a girl. I just want
a healthy baby.*

*It makes no difference to me - but I know
my husband would love to have a little girl.*

*I just want to know the sex in advance so
that I can prepare the baby's room
appropriately.*

*It really doesn't matter, but how cool would
it be to take my daughter to get our nails and
hair done together.*

*Practically, if you have a son at least you
don't have to worry about them getting
pregnant as a teen.*

*I just know he would be a very protective
father to a little girl.
She would be his delicate little flower.*

*Having a boy would mean having lots of
wild energy and mess all of the time.*

I had similar thoughts myself. I wanted a boy
– because I understood about being a girl and
I feared a daughter might become as sensitive
as me and that made me worry for her

happiness. At least with a son I had no assumptions that I would know what I was doing!

From the very instant that you understand the sex of your unborn baby, your world changes.

The mental images that quickly and unconsciously form upon hearing, 'It's a girl', or, 'It's a boy!' will vary greatly. These initial images are influenced by your own cultural bias and upbringing, and your awareness of what impact they have on you.

When the Japanese doctor announced, 'You have a boy!', there was a brief moment of confusion where I had no idea which gender my baby was as he used a word I had not yet learned.

For that brief moment, the slate was clean. I could not attach 'blue or pink' to that precious human that was just beginning the journey of life.

It was simply a baby. Pure and innocent and ours.

I now understand that with the announcement that we had a boy, I was destined to travel down a path that would change my world in ways I could not have imagined.

Parents are faced with two options: continue to raise their son as society dictates and expects you to or begin the search for what is truly best for your son and what you can do to ensure that.

This book is for the second group.

You don't know what you don't know!

I felt driven to delve deeper into learning and gaining a better understanding. The more I learned, the more I realized how much I did not know and was not aware of!

Something amazing happens when you give birth to a boy.

As a woman, you are giving birth to the other half of humanity. You have some understanding of what it means to be your half of the human race, but you really don't have a clear idea of what it feels like to be in the world as a male.

Everything you know is through the eyes of a woman.

You have some beliefs and understandings about males but you have never had this intimate of a relationship with one as you are now starting with your son's birth.

You have brought this male into the world.

You are responsible to raise him the best that you can.

How are you going to do it?

You need to understand what challenges your son will face simply having been born a male; to become knowledgeable about what really goes on in the world of a male, not simply what he chooses to show you and what you choose to see. You have to become your son's biggest champion, your boy's strongest advocate.

In general, males are more likely to be diagnosed with a behaviour disorder, prescribed stimulant medications, fail out of school, binge drink, commit a violent crime, and/or take their own lives. Let's look at a few disturbing statistics about males:

❖ In many countries, the suicide rate for men is two to three times higher than among women. Girls may have more suicide attempts, and boys have more suicide completions. In the US, around 35,000 men die by suicide each year; about one death every 15 minutes. In Canada, approximately 3,000 men die by suicide per year, translating to over 50 deaths per week.

❖ Boys are twice as likely to drop out of school and four times as likely to be expelled, in comparison to girls. In North America, 30% more boys are likely to drop out of school.

❖ Boys constitute 65% of special-ed. students, and are five times more likely to be labeled as hyperactive, and four times more likely to be diagnosed with ADHD.

❖ Boys are more likely to receive school suspensions and expulsions, with estimates varying but often exceeding 60 to 70% of disciplinary actions involving boys.

❖ Boys comprise around 70 to 80%of the juvenile detention population.

We never think that these statistics might include our sons. We can't imagine our sweet little boys ending up on a path marked with addiction, violence, depression or even suicide. It's beyond our imagination to see our sons behind bars. But, it can happen. It has happened. To parents who believed it could never happen. It can happen to any one of us.

I believe that when we are more aware of the inner world of boys we can provide a nurturing environment where our sons can grow up and help them become more attuned to the pressures of the world around them. We have the ability to share with them these statistics and talk about what might be behind them. We can talk about a new healthy image of masculinity.

In my world, there are many good, admirable men who have faced a challenging path, and maybe with greater awareness, they could have avoided paying such a heavy emotional toll for simply being born male.

There are also men who perpetuate harmful stereotypes and contribute to the concept of toxic masculinity. They regularly make the headlines or are center stage in stories we hear from our friends. They exist. But maybe they just didn't have a way out.

I believe our boys deserve better.

I believe that once you understand the power you have as a parent in creating a safe, loving environment for your son to grow up in, then, perhaps, you will be part of the movement that breaks down the Boy Code.

Your son will have a chance to develop a strong, holistic emotional world and will understand that he can become a remarkable man.

But he needs you to do your part. For him.

Let's start together to learn what needs to be learnt and then act upon it.

Let's begin this journey to become a champion for your boys, for all boys.

## *Parenting Paradigm Shift*

## *This Quiz Can Change Everything*

Start your journey of self-discovery by taking this comprehensive Gender Bias Quiz @ oasis.col.org. This interactive quiz will unveil your own hidden gender biases and shed light on the ways societal expectations and stereotypes may have influenced your perceptions.

After completing and scoring the quiz, you'll receive recommendations for further steps to take on your path towards gender bias awareness.

You will be able to dive deeper into the topic with additional information and eye-opening charts that illuminate the pervasive nature of gender discrimination throughout life.

Expand your awareness and understanding of how gender biases are impacting how you are parenting your son. Once you gain awareness, everything has the potential to change, both for you and your son.

This is perhaps the most challenging aspect of my work. Some of our unconscious beliefs are so deeply ingrained that we remain blind to them. But make no mistake - they do impact how we parent our children. I truly believed that I understood about stereotyping and biases, and felt rather confident and proud that I could see things objectively. If I had not experienced the fishing experience when our son was three, the event that turned everything upside down for me, I would never have embarked on this journey. I had no idea of what I didn't know about boys, and the insights missing from my parenting. I am so grateful that day happened and that I was able to reflect on it, realizing that something was terribly wrong with how I had reacted. By reading this book, you can start on the path much sooner than I did.

# *Let's talk about The Boy Code*

As we start down this path of discovery, the first place we need to examine is ourselves.

Our belief system about gender is deeply ingrained and often unconscious. It comes from how we were raised ourselves, what society then told us were the acceptable roles for males and females, and role models we had in our life.

Many people never think to challenge these deeply rooted, often unconscious expectations we hold for ourselves, and then, for our children. As a result, these expectations persist and continue to be passed down through generations.

The main messages found within the Boy Code are:

**Boys will be boys.**
Boys are naturally aggressive due to testosterone.

**Boys should be boys.**
Only anger is an acceptable emotion.
Don't show any weakness or vulnerability.

**Boys are toxic.**
They are dangerous to society.

The Boy Code is societal expectations for a boy to conform to traditional masculine ideals.

Boys may feel pressured to hide vulnerability and mask their true emotions to fit into these ideals.

The book, *Real Boys: Rescuing Our Sons from the Myths of Boyhood,* became the catalyst for a lifetime of searching for ways to make the world better for boys, and for their parents.

Dr. William Pollack first spoke in his book about the Boy Code in 1999, based on decades of researching the inner lives of boys.

*Pollack challenges conventional expectations about manhood and masculinity that encourage parents to treat boys as little men, raising them through a toughening process that drives their true emotions underground. Only when we understand what boys are really like, says Pollack, can we help them develop more self-confidence and the emotional savvy they need to deal with issues such as depression, love and sexuality, drugs and alcohol, divorce, and violence.*
*(excerpt from Amazon book description)*

Society sends mixed messages about what it means to be a man. Outwardly many men wear the masks we expect to see while on the inside many of them are sad, lonely and confused. Pollack speaks about boys' self-esteem, the power of parents, how to communicate with boys more effectively, depression, and so much more. His book was my initial introduction into the inner emotional world of boys, nearly twenty-five years ago. His book concluded with a request for the reader: Spread The Word.

That became my mission.

34

# *The Tender Years (0~3)*

## *Perspectives*

### The Parents' View

Parenting during the first three years of your son's life is an extraordinary and transformative experience. Through the sleepless nights, milestones reached, and cherished moments, you become the guiding force in your child's life. The love, care, and attention you provide during this critical period lay the foundation for their growth, development, and future success.

The first three years of a child's life are a time of incredible growth and development – for both the child and the parent! It can be a bit overwhelming at times.

It begins with a familiar pattern of sleepless nights, diaper changes, and round-the-clock feeding during the infancy stage. As time progresses, the journey includes the challenges of toddlerhood, where power struggles intertwine with the joys of witnessing your son emerge as his own, unique individual. These first years are a marvel to behold, as his growth unfolds at a miraculous speed.

Your world will never be the same. You will never be the same. You are responsible for another human being. And he is watching absolutely everything as he is making sense of this new world and finding his place in it. He is learning to be a boy.

This book will help you become aware of gender bias, even if you haven't uncovered it yet. It will enhance your understanding of gender differences and provide you with valuable tools and strategies for parenting. It will help you create a strong and deep relationship right from the start. It will change your perspective about raising your son and that will impact how you parent him. It will give your son the best possible chance of growing into a remarkable man, with a healthy inner emotional world.

## The Mother's View

Many of us pass through these initial years in a bit of a blur. Your emotions are often all over the place - a whirlwind of love, joy, protectiveness, and those occasional moments of overwhelm and uncertainty.

From the moment you hold your baby boy in your arms for the first time, an overwhelming surge of love washes over you, creating an unbreakable bond that grows stronger with each passing day. The feelings of protectiveness and fierce devotion come naturally to you, as you become his primary source of care and comfort.

As you navigate the challenges of infancy, you experience a mixture of exhaustion and elation. The early days are marked by an intense focus on your son's needs, as you learn to decipher his cries and cues, striving to meet every need and soothe his tiny heart. At the same time, you recognize the importance of both parents being aligned in a collaborative approach to raising your son.

You wrestle with your own doubts and insecurities, wondering if you are doing everything right and if you are enough for your son. Mother guilt and insecurity often knock at your door.

As your son enters the toddler years, you witness an explosion of curiosity and independence, and big emotions. As his parents, you may grapple with the challenges of setting boundaries and handling his tantrums. You start to get a glimpse of how the world sees your boy, and the messages that are being sent. You begin to confront the impact of the Boy Code.

It is a time of learning for both mother and son as you navigate the evolving dynamics of your relationship and the relationship your son is developing in the larger world he is becoming a part of. You find yourself shaping your own understanding of what it means to be a mother raising a boy in a world that is constantly evolving around him.

## The Father's View

There is nothing in the world that can truly prepare you for the life-altering moment when your son arrives. As you stand witness to your wife's body expanding to accommodate this new life, it's as if you're glimpsing a miracle unfolding before your eyes. Yet, despite its beauty, the profound impact this little being will have on your world remains beyond your grasp.

Amidst the overwhelming joy that fills your heart, there are moments of doubt and uncertainty that creep in. The weight of responsibility for this precious little boy feels like a heavy burden, and you find yourself pondering how to fulfill your duties as a father and husband, ensuring a life of happiness and love for both your son and your wife.

From the moment you hear his first cries, you are struck with a deep sense of awe at the miracle of life. But there's also a tinge of uncertainty as you gaze at this tiny, fragile creature in your arms. You can't help but feel a bit clumsy and unsure of yourself, especially when compared to your wife, who has been nurturing and caring for him for nine months within her body. She seems to know exactly what to do, having read every parenting book on the shelf.

You do your best to support and help, but as the days go by, you sometimes feel like a third wheel in this new adventure of parenthood. Your wife appears to be a completely different person, radiating with maternal instinct and confidence. Meanwhile, you are left wondering whether your efforts are truly helpful or just a hindrance.

Feeling a bit lost and confused, you yearn for guidance and reassurance in this new role as a father. You want to be the best dad possible for your son, to be there for him through every step of his journey, and to create a bond that will last a lifetime. You simply are not sure how to accomplish this.

## The Son's View

From the moment you enter this world, everything seems vast and unfamiliar. Fragile and dependent, you rely on your parents for your every need. The world presents itself as a vibrant tapestry of colors, sounds, and sensations that stimulate your developing senses. You feel the warmth of embraces, the steady rhythm of loved ones' heartbeats as they nestle you in their arms. It is a time of pure innocence and wonder as you embark on the journey of life.

As you grow older, your curiosity also grows, fueling an insatiable thirst for knowledge. Your explorations begin, reaching out to touch and interact with the world around you. Every object you encounter becomes a source of fascination, from the softness of a stuffed animal to the coolness of a shiny toy. You marvel at movements and sounds, attempting to make sense of this vast and dynamic world.

Social interactions start to become important to you. Laughter makes you happy, and being embraced by loved ones makes you feel safe. You long for attention and affection, wanting to be seen, approved of, and cheered on. Our smiles and praise mean everything to you as you eagerly try to have us recognize even your smallest accomplishments.

But it isn't all rainbows and unicorns. Challenges and frustrations also occupy your world, testing your patience and resilience. You struggle to articulate your needs and desires, sometimes resorting to cries and tantrums when words fail you.

Explosive emotions can result from what appears to be the smallest of triggers. You often experience moments of anger and confusion, grappling with the unpredictability of the world. It is a time of emotional highs and lows, navigating a range of feelings without a compass.

Throughout these years, you are in a constant state of learning and adaptation. The world gradually reveals its societal rules and expectations, shaping your self-perception and understanding of your place in the world.

You become aware of some of the nuances of the distinct roles assigned to boys and girls, sensing subtle differences in treatment. Society's expectations are molding you into a future man, even before you fully grasp what that really means.

Reflecting upon these formative years, it becomes clear that they lay the foundation for your development. They are the stepping stones that contribute to shaping your identity, influencing your perspectives, and molding your perception of yourself and others. It is a time of growth, discovery, and self-awareness.

# *Bias from the beginning*

You have found your soulmate, the love of your life, and are creating a future together. Before long, there is a family addition – a baby is born!

Celebration! Excitement! Pivot!

Transition from being a happy couple into the role of caregiver and protector.

You both are now responsible for this little bundle and how you parent him will impact how he sees himself. That is quite a daunting realization.

Your encounters with males, be it within your family, friends, or through media, shape your perception of the male species and what it means to be male. Whether you grew up with brothers, sisters, or as an only child, the way you were raised leaves an indelible mark on you, whether you realize it or not. Your father, as the first significant male figure in your life, holds a lasting place in your memory. As you raise your own son, will you adhere to that version of manhood, or will you make a solemn vow to raise him differently?

Can you reflect on those things that influenced you growing up and connect the dots to how that helped create your understanding of gender? Can you be intentional in what you want to continue to impact you and what you do not need anymore?

Will you be able to spot the ways that gender bias, those stereotypical expectations, is evident in our society, and in your own world? Are you willing to look for them?

Babies are babies; they are so small, so precious, so innocent. You might assume they are all treated the same. You would be wrong.

Studies have been done. Data confirms it.

Even at the time of birth, how a baby is reacted to, held, spoken to and comforted differs depending on whether it is a boy or a girl baby.

The occurrence of this phenomenon is not limited to just hospital staff; parents also display this behavior. What is particularly concerning is that many individuals are unaware that they are engaging in this behavior. Without recognizing the need for change, it is difficult to bring about any significant improvements. Although the extent of the impact on infants when they are treated differently based on their gender is unclear, it is certain that there is an effect.

In an ideal world, it would be valuable if, before becoming parents, we were mandated to undergo a process, such as the quiz found earlier in this section. This process could help to unearth our unconscious prejudices and stereotypical beliefs. By participating in this process, we would gain insight into the influences shaping our perceptions of males and females, including societal norms, media portrayals, and the attitudes of our friends and family.

Armed with this knowledge, we would be better equipped to raise our boys. Society imposes an unwritten set of rules known as "The Boy Code". It perpetuates the notion that boys will inevitably behave in certain ways due to their testosterone levels, and it dictates which male behaviors are deemed acceptable and stoic, while branding others as weak, feminine, and unacceptable. Regrettably, the message implied is that boys are inherently toxic.

None of us likely aspire to raise our boys under the weight of such implicit expectations. However, this is often the reality we face. In order to foster progress, we must first acknowledge the challenges that our boys encounter in the world. Additionally, we must critically examine our own actions, whether intentional or unintentional, that contribute to perpetuating this cycle. Only then can we hope to witness a transformation in the experiences of our boys.

Maybe, like me, you think this doesn't apply to you; that you are conscious of your beliefs and aware of stereotypes. I challenge you to dig deeper and uncover what you don't even know exists right now. You will be shocked, and uncovering that will greatly impact your parenting. You have nothing to lose, and your son has everything to gain.

In an experiment known as "Girl toys vs boy toys," researchers at BBC aimed to investigate if slightly older toddlers were treated differently based on their gender.

The selected participants claimed to be impartial and to treat all children equally, without any gender biases.

For the experiment, the toddlers' clothing was secretly swapped to make the girls appear more boyish and vice versa. This made it impossible for the children to be identified as either gender, except for their clothing. The children were then placed in a room with a range of toys that were typically associated with boys or girls.

When a new adult entered the room with the sole intention of playing with the child, it was not surprising that the toys offered to the child were based on the assumed gender.

When the adult believed the toddler was a boy, boy-type toys were given and the play was more aggressive with harsher language, compared to when the adult thought the toddler was a girl.

The most valuable insight gleaned from this experiment was that all adults were shocked to discover they had reacted to the child based on their perceived gender. Their eyes were opened!

When you are not aware, you will perpetuate the problem!

One of the primary objectives of this book is to raise parents' awareness so that, from the very beginning of your son's life, you can understand how others, and even yourself, interact with boys.

Another reason is to inspire and encourage you to challenge societal norms and break free from the confines of the "Boy Code".  Through exploring the material in this book, you will gain the understanding and tools to encourage your sons to embrace their authentic selves, cultivating a sense of confidence and resilience that will carry them through life.

When we take the time to really dive into our boys' world, we can start to grasp the whole picture and understand what's really going on. And once we have that understanding, we can work towards creating an environment where our boys are not just accepted, but truly cherished.

In essence, this book is meant to be a powerful resource for parents who are eager to understand their boys on a deeper level and create an environment where their unique qualities are recognized and respected. It is an invitation to embark on a transformative journey that will have a lasting impact on your life and the lives of the males in your world.

## *Building The Foundation*

# These Golden Years

*"The development of the
child during the first three
years after birth is unequaled
in intensity and importance by
any period that precedes or
follows in the whole life of the
child."*

Maria Montessori

You are walking through the park, your little bundle of joy gazing up at you from the pram, when you notice the children playing in the big sandbox just off the strolling path. You decide to take a break and sit on the bench with your small son, and just enjoy watching the children play.

You are thinking, in amazement, that only a few years down the road your little guy could be doing the same thing, playing happily with other little boys in that sandbox.

You notice one boy, somewhere between 3 and 4, and you start to feel uneasy.

This little boy becomes more and more aggressive, almost like a mean little bully. He relentlessly demands the toy truck another boy is playing with, becoming increasingly forceful. The timid child holds onto the truck tightly, until the aggressive boy loses control and hits him with a shovel, snatching the truck away.

In response to the injured boy's cries, both mothers rush over to the sandbox. While one mother consoles her hurt child, the other lightly scolds her son. But then, something happens that surprises you. She looks at the other mom, rolls her eyes, and nonchalantly remarks, "boys will be boys."

In that moment, a mix of emotions swirl within you. You feel sympathy for the hurt child and frustration towards the aggressive behavior, but also a sense of disappointment at the mother's response. It's as if she's brushing off her son's actions as if they are inevitable or expected, using the old saying as a justification. This is the Boy Code in action.

As you gaze down at the little bundle in your arms, the significance of your role as a parent becomes even more apparent. You begin to envision the impact that your parenting will have on your son in the years to come. And one thing becomes crystal clear – this is not the way you intend to raise your son.

The initial three years of a child's life are often regarded as the most vital because it sets the foundation for everything that follows. During this time, a child develops their sense of safety and security; their understanding that the world is a good place and that they are safe, loved and cared for. It is the grass roots of their self-esteem; they start to learn more about being resilient, how to love being alive.

These initial years play a critical role in ensuring that your son grows up to be a confident, caring, and happy child, which is why it is imperative that we prioritize this time. As conscious and intentional parents, it is our responsibility to shape our child's foundation during these formative years. Many cultures, including Japan, have proverbs emphasizing the importance of this time, as did Maria Montessori. In Japan, it is believed that the soul of a three-year-old persists until the age of one hundred.

# Years of Incredible Growth

If you could witness a time-lapse of your son's growth, from a tiny newborn to a vibrant and lively three-year-old, it would be nothing short of astonishing. The incredible transformation that takes place in such a short span of time would leave you in awe.

As his parents, you bear a weighty responsibility. Your child's world revolves around you and the environment you create for him. You hold the power to shape his reality, providing him with a sense of safety, love, and belonging within your family.

With each passing day, your son becomes more independent, and his world expands. It can feel like a constant challenge to keep pace with his ever-changing needs and interests. Just when you think you understand this newfound sense of curiosity and exploration, he surprises you with new developments, and you find yourself adapting once again.

He watches you and takes in absolutely everything you do and say and feel. Before you will be able to confirm this, before he can verbalize it, he will be absorbing it all. You are his primary role model, and he is soaking up every experience and interaction.

Throughout the twos and threes, you will be amazed at the magnitude of his emotions, the boundless energy he possesses, and the fact that you are keeping up with him!

Despite the challenges, you will be totally captivated by what a kind, sweet boy you have.

His world will still be very much your world.

## *Communication*

During the first three years of a child's life, language and communication development is of utmost importance. This is because the brain is highly receptive to learning during this period, undergoing rapid growth and forming essential neural connections for language. It relies on billions of neurons creating connections, known as synapses, to facilitate the transmission of information.

Specific regions of the brain are dedicated to language processing, production, and comprehension. Throughout these critical years, these language-related brain areas experience substantial growth and specialization, laying the groundwork for your child's linguistic journey.

As his parents, your interactions and engagement with your child during this crucial period play a profound role in shaping their brain development. Surround your child with a language-rich environment, immersing him in a world filled with diverse vocabulary, captivating stories, and meaningful social interactions. Engaging in meaningful conversations, reading stories together, and participating in enjoyable language activities all contribute to nurturing their linguistic skills and forming vital neural connections. By creating an optimal environment for your child's brain to flourish, you are laying the foundation for their lifelong language and communication abilities.

In those magical first months, your son begins to recognize and respond to the sounds and voices that envelop him. He listens intently, his bright eyes following your every movement. As he watches and listens, he starts to build connections between the sounds he hears and the people and objects in his environment.

Soon, you'll notice the emergence of adorable babbling and cooing. These delightful vocalizations are his way of experimenting with the art of communication. During this time, you play a pivotal role as his first language models. As you engage in loving interactions, talk to him, and respond to his coos and babbles, you provide him with the rich language input he needs to develop his own communication skills.

By the second year in your little boy's life, there is a linguistic growth spurt. This is a period filled with exciting leaps and bounds in language development and communication. During this time, your little guy undergoes a linguistic metamorphosis, transforming from a babbling baby into a budding communicator.

It's a remarkable journey to witness as he gains a growing command of words and begins to express himself with increasing clarity.

As your son embarks on his second year, you'll notice an explosion of vocabulary. Words become his trusty companions, and he starts to use them to communicate his wants, needs, and curiosities. He joyfully experiments with language, mimicking the sounds and words he hears from those around him.

Your son starts to grasp the meaning behind words and instructions, responding appropriately to simple requests. You might be pleasantly surprised by his ability to follow directions, whether it's putting away his toys or finding his favorite stuffed animal.

Your little boy begins to develop social communication skills, such as turn-taking in conversation and understanding social cues. He starts to pick up on nonverbal communication, like facial expressions and body language, which enhance his ability to connect and interact with others.

By the time your son reaches his third year, his language skills continue to blossom at an impressive pace. He becomes increasingly adept at using words and constructing more complex sentences. You'll witness his vocabulary expanding as he eagerly absorbs new words.

At this stage, your little boy begins to express his thoughts, feelings, and desires with increasing clarity. He learns to articulate his needs, preferences, and experiences, allowing you to better understand his world. This newfound ability to communicate enables him to interact more meaningfully with others, forging connections and building relationships.

He can now understand and follow simple instructions, respond to questions, and engage in back-and-forth exchanges. This lays the groundwork for effective communication and cooperative play with peers, setting the stage for future social interactions.

These are the years when the foundation is laid. When parents are intentional from the start in creating a literacy rich and stimulating environment, boys can pass through these stages of language and communication development with great success.

It begins with absorbing sounds and voices, then progresses to building vocabulary, and constructing more complex sentences.

Conversational skills and social awareness blossom during this time.

Boys may face different challenges that make it even more critical to make these early years as language rich as possible.

Studies suggest that differences in language-related regions of the brain and connectivity patterns can contribute to boys lagging behind girls in early language development. The brain is a remarkably flexible organ, capable of adapting and rewiring itself in response to experiences and environmental factors. A boy's early environment and experiences impact his language development.

Creating an environment that fosters language growth and providing ample opportunities for communication is vital for setting a strong foundation for a boy's language journey.

Why might boys experience challenges in their language development compared to girls during the early years?

❖ **Brain Differences:** Studies have found that there are subtle differences in brain structure and function between boys and girls. Some research suggests that girls may have a slight advantage in areas associated with language processing and verbal abilities.

❖ **Developmental Timing:** Boys may exhibit a slight delay in language development compared to girls, particularly in the early stages. This delay tends to level out as they grow older, but it can create a gap during the early years.

❖ **Parental Interaction**: Studies have shown that parents may engage in different types of interactions with boys and girls, which can impact language development. For example, parents may engage in more conversational and expressive language with girls, while using directive and action-based language with boys. This difference in interaction styles may contribute to variations in language skills.

❖ **Environmental Factors**: Environmental factors, such as exposure to language-rich environments, access to books, and opportunities for verbal interaction, play a crucial role in language development. Boys who have limited exposure to these factors may not have the same opportunities for language stimulation as girls, which can impact their language skills.

❖ Social Expectations: Societal expectations and stereotypes about gender roles can influence language development. Boys may face pressures to conform to traditional masculine norms, which can discourage expressive and verbal behaviors. This, in turn, may impact their language development.

We can impact our son's language development and communication skills by being aware of possible challenges and intentionally providing the environment that will support his growth. Focusing on creating a language-rich environment, providing ample opportunities for communication and verbal interaction, and challenging gender stereotypes can help support our boys' language development and bridge any gaps that may arise.

Throughout your son's entire life, the most critical factor in staying connected is how you learn to communicate with each other. Put communication as a top priority in your child rearing practices and you will better weather the many challenges that will arise throughout his life. Here are a few points to keep in mind:

**Start early:** Little boys may face challenges in understanding emotional vocabulary, so begin as soon as possible. Talk about what you're doing and feeling in natural, everyday ways. Even before your son can participate verbally, he'll absorb everything you say.

**Identify emotions:** Play games to help your son identify emotions. For example, read people's expressions and talk about what might be behind their emotions. Create stories to go with the emotions you see on people's faces. This can help your son understand and express his emotions better.

**Provide quality resources:** Offer your son books and videos that have high emotional content and values you want to instill in him. I remember (many moons ago) falling in love with a series of books and videos called The Land Before Time that explored a wide range of emotions. It had a strong attraction for a little boy curious about dinosaurs and experiencing his own world of emotions.

**Connect behavior to emotions:** When your son has a tantrum, connect his behavior to emotions and discuss what may have caused them. For example, talk about the big feelings he showed and what might have been behind them. Connect the fact that he put up resistance at bedtime the night before, so maybe he didn't get enough sleep. This can help him understand his emotions better and learn how to manage them. If your son really does understand, don't be surprised if sometime down the road, when you have reacted in a bit of a tantrum yourself, he asks you if that happened because you didn't get enough sleep. It happened to me. They take it all in!

**Boost self-esteem:** Girls often are much more articulate and have a real command over language from a young age. It might be easy for a little boy to feel he is not as good as the girl. He might become quite frustrated or angry when he feels overpowered by the girl's fluid language capacity. His self-esteem might need some building-up opportunities for verbal sharing. Being aware of this possible roadblock in communication can greatly impact how your son feels about himself.

Effective communication is the foundation for building a strong relationship with your son. As your son grows, continue to prioritize communication and adapt your strategies to his changing needs. With a strong foundation in communication, you can navigate the challenges of parenthood and enjoy a deep, fulfilling connection with your son.

# *Behaviour*

The early years of a child's life are an important time for setting expectations around behaviour. During this period, their brain is highly receptive to external experiences that can influence the way they think, behave, and learn. Interactions with caregivers and the environment play a vital role in developing important skills like empathy, self-control, and communication.

Positive interactions that promote healthy development can have a profound impact on a child's social and emotional skills. When children consistently experience nurturing and supportive interactions, they are more likely to develop positive behavior patterns and strong social-emotional abilities.

Conversely, negative or inconsistent interactions can lead to the development of negative behavior patterns, such as aggression or anxiety. That's why it is vital for parents and caregivers to provide a nurturing and stable environment during these formative years. By doing so, they can establish a foundation for positive behavior patterns that can have long-lasting effects throughout a child's life.

Every parent approaches what is commonly called 'The Terrible Twos & The Trying Threes' with some apprehension. This is a time when children are testing boundaries and asserting their independence, which can lead to some intense moments. Many parents can relate to stories of feeling overwhelmed or losing their composure during this stage.

Believe me, it can bring even the strongest of us to our knees!

Even with the best intentions, I vividly recall a moment when I was pushed to my limits just before my son turned three. I can't quite remember what triggered the tantrum, but I certainly remember the overwhelming emotions I experienced.

They were not nice, they were not motherly.

My feelings seemed even bigger than his! I tried all my tricks, but nothing worked to help him pass through the tantrum.

I felt exhausted, frustrated, angry, incompetent - anything but Mom of the Year.

And then I was scared because I knew I was at a dangerous point. A point where I might do or say something I would regret. I also knew I was the adult in the room.

So, I decided to give myself a Time Out.

I walked over to the kitchen counter, and dropped my head into my arms. I needed to get control of myself. As the tears of frustration began to fall, I consciously made myself take deeper breaths. I put every ounce of willpower into those breaths, creating a barrier to my little guys screams and tugs on my legs. I laser focused on counting four breaths in, hold for four, and out for six. It was a struggle, but I could feel the shift in my emotions almost immediately.

As I regained control of my emotions, I sat on the floor and opened my arms to my son. He rushed into my arms, and together, we shared a moment of release. More tears were shed, but through the magical power of hugs, we found solace and were able to move forward, connected and comforted.

I don't believe in Time Out for children, but I think it can be a very wise strategy for us parents when we have just reached our limit.

There's a lot going on in toddlerhood!

It's a wild and wonderful world. It's a time of immense growth and exploration, where boys often experience a disconnect between their intellectual understanding and their behavior.

This can lead to frustration, and sometimes that frustration finds its expression in physical outbursts or meltdowns.

But here's the thing: it's crucial not to get too fixated on the behavior alone. Every instance of misbehavior is an opportunity for us as parents to become detectives and explore the hidden emotions behind our child's actions. Instead of simply reacting to the behavior, we can approach it with curiosity and a genuine desire to understand what happened and why. What triggered the tantrum? What lies beneath the surface?

When our little ones display challenging behavior, it's essential to remember that their actions are often a reflection of an underlying emotion or need not being met. Perhaps they are feeling overwhelmed, frustrated, scared, or even seeking attention. By taking a moment to step back and observe, we can start unraveling the mystery behind their behavior.

When your little boy has a major meltdown in the store because you said no to that tempting candy bar, it's important to recognize that it's not a sign of him being a "bad" or intentionally defiant child. There may be various factors at play. Is he close to his nap time, feeling hungry or thirsty, struggling to express himself, overwhelmed by too much stimulation, or simply brimming with pent-up energy?

Or if your son throws a tantrum because you told him it's time to leave the park, take a pause before responding. Get curious about what might be going on beneath the surface. Is he having difficulty transitioning from one activity to another? Does he feel a sense of loss or disappointment in leaving a place he enjoys? Is he seeking more control or autonomy in his choices?

By exploring the hidden emotions driving the behavior, we can respond with empathy and understanding, offering comfort and guidance. It's an opportunity to teach our children valuable emotional regulation skills and provide them with tools to express their feelings in a more constructive manner.

Being curious about the hidden emotions behind misbehavior also helps foster a deeper connection with our children. It shows them that we genuinely care about their well-being and are invested in understanding their experiences. This open and empathetic approach strengthens the parent-child bond, creating an environment of trust and emotional safety.

Remember, your son is still in the process of learning that he can't always have or do everything he desires. He's navigating the complexities of life, and it's our responsibility as parents to guide him along this path. It's unnecessary to make him feel terrible for causing a scene. Instead, we can help him understand the consequences of his behavior and teach him the importance of taking responsibility for his actions.

Keep in mind that uncovering the hidden emotions behind misbehavior is not always a straightforward task. It requires active listening, observation, and ongoing communication with your child. Some situations may require patience and multiple conversations to fully grasp the root cause. But through this process of exploration and understanding, we can provide our children with the support and guidance they need to navigate their emotions and behavior more effectively.

In the early years, before your child can articulate and explain their emotions and needs, there will be moments when it falls solely on you as a parent to trust that they are doing the best they can in that moment. It's crucial to remember that there is always a reason behind their misbehavior, even if you can't immediately figure it out.

During these times, your role is to be a source of unwavering support for your child. Recognize that they may be overwhelmed by big emotions they struggle to express or understand. It's your loving presence and empathetic guidance that will help them navigate through these challenging moments.

Instead of resorting to frustration or punishment, approach your child with an open heart and mind. Show them that you trust in their inherent goodness and that you're there to help them through their struggles. Offer reassurance and understanding, letting them know that it's okay to feel the way they do.

In general, when it comes to guiding boys, a fair, firm, and consistent approach tends to be effective. Research has shown that boys benefit from clear boundaries and routines. They feel more secure when they know what is expected of them and understand the consequences of their actions. This fosters a sense of safety and predictability, helping them navigate the world with greater confidence.

As you guide your child through their big emotions, model the behaviors you want them to develop. Show them how to regulate their own emotions by managing your own reactions calmly and compassionately. By demonstrating empathy and love, you create an environment that fosters emotional growth and resilience.

Embracing this approach to misbehavior does not imply becoming a permissive parent. It means being consistent in guiding your son on social skills and emotional regulation. It's important not to simply let children behave without guidance and support. Instead, we provide them with the necessary tools, skills and strategies to understand and embody kindness and compassion, shaping them into empathetic and well-rounded individuals, eventually becoming remarkable men.

When it comes to helping boys understand and regulate their behavior, there are some tried and true strategies that can make a difference:

**Role model** - he watches EVERYTHING you do, so make sure you are modeling the behaviors you want to instill in him. He is soaking up everything in his environment. If you want him to be kind and gentle, make sure that is how he sees you interacting with others. If you want him to control his anger outburst, don't explode when someone cuts you off while you are driving. Show him how to resolve conflicts peacefully, apologize when necessary, and engage in positive social interactions. By being a positive role model, you provide him with a blueprint for navigating social situations and developing healthy relationships.

**Notice and comment on the good**. It is easy to feel like you are constantly saying 'No!' or 'Stop that!' or similar comments. Be sure to find times that you can say things like, 'Wow, that was such a kind thing to do.' or 'That was being really responsible to put all those things back in their spot.' or 'That was a hard thing to tell me - you should be very proud that you were so honest with me.' By specifically highlighting his positive actions, you reinforce those behaviors and boost his self-esteem. There are a variety of parent tips around this but one I prefer is the idea that for every 1 negative comment or interaction you make sure to find 7 positive ones. Keep your son's Emotional Bank full.

**Empower your son** any time it is possible. Give your son opportunities to make choices and take on age-appropriate responsibilities. Let him have a say in certain decisions, encourage his independence, and involve him in chores or tasks he can handle. Empowering him fosters confidence and a sense of autonomy. Anything a child can do for himself, he should do by himself (even if he takes forever to do it!).

**Talk to him honestly** about your feelings. Open and honest conversations with your son build trust and emotional connection. Share your own feelings and experiences, including moments when you made mistakes and learned from them. For instance, you can say, "I felt really frustrated earlier because I didn't get enough sleep. I'm sorry if I snapped at you. It's important to take care of ourselves so we can be kind to each other." By modeling vulnerability and expressing love, you create a safe space for him to understand and express his own emotions.

**Set clear limits.** Establishing clear boundaries is crucial for your son's understanding of expectations and appropriate behavior. For instance, if you've established a "no whining" rule, remind him, in a calm tone, to use a normal voice when expressing his needs. Be consistent in enforcing the boundaries you set, and ensure there are consequences for breaking important rules. Pick your battles wisely, focusing on the most important rules while allowing some flexibility.

**Embrace humor and imagination.** Infusing humor and imagination into your interactions can make learning and behavior management more enjoyable. Create playful games, engage in imaginative play together, and find opportunities to laugh and have fun as a family. For example, turn a chore like tidying up into a game where you pretend to be superheroes organizing their secret lair. By incorporating humor and imagination, you create a positive and joyful environment that fosters connection and engagement.

**Support language development.** Understand that language skills may develop at different rates for boys, and it's important to provide a supportive environment. Surround him with age-appropriate books, engage in conversations, sing songs, and encourage him to express himself. For instance, ask open-ended questions, such as "What was your favorite part of the day?" or "Tell me about the picture you drew." Actively listen and respond attentively to his attempts at communication, reinforcing his language development and boosting his confidence.

It is easy to forget that our toddler boys are still very young. When your little guy turns two years old he has only been on this planet for 730 days. Think about that! And look what has already happened in only 730 days. Bit of a miracle.

It is during these precious years that we, as parents, have an incredible opportunity to lay the groundwork for the remarkable stages that lie ahead. By nurturing our children's social and emotional development, empowering them with love and guidance, and cherishing each milestone they achieve, we create a solid foundation for their future.

With love and guidance, we can shape the boundless potential within our growing boys, and watch the chaos become harmony.

# *Boys In Focus:*

# *Raising Awareness*

As you bring your precious little baby boy home from the hospital, your primary responsibilities as a parent revolve around providing him with love, care, and meeting his basic needs.

As your son grows and develops his own distinct personality, you might begin to observe disparities between your assumptions about male behaviour and your son's actual actions. Your preconceived ideas of an energetic wild young boy might face a test when you realize how emotionally sensitive he is. It might upset you a bit if he is too scared to continue to watch a Disney movie while his girl-friend of the same age is thoroughly enjoying it all. Even worse if someone actually tells him to toughen up, like her.

As his world begins to expand, your son may start to have experiences that leave him feeling confused. He may begin to experience the realities of the Boy Code.

At the park, you may observe that your son, like many other little boys, possesses a boundless amount of physical energy compared to his female counterparts. It is natural and necessary for young boys to have ample opportunities to explore, engage in physical activities, and use their bodies actively. However, this abundance of energy can sometimes cause concern and even uneasiness among parents of little girls, who may feel protective and cautious about potential interactions.

Your son may come across messages and social cues that he may not fully grasp, but he can still sense them on an emotional level. For instance, while racing around the park, if he accidentally bumps into a little girl and witnesses her mother reacting with anger or disapproval, he might not fully comprehend the intricacies of the situation. But he can still pick up on the emotions involved and may develop a sense that the girl's mother does not like him or want him to interact with her daughter. It is crucial to keep in mind that even young children are perceptive and can absorb these subtle emotional dynamics, which shape their understanding of social interactions.

Such experiences can create confusion for a young boy as he tries to make sense of the mixed messages he receives about his behavior and interactions with others. The subtle cues and societal expectations associated with gender can inadvertently perpetuate stereotypes and reinforce the "Boy

Code," which dictates how boys should act and behave. This can leave a young boy feeling unsure about how to navigate social interactions and may impact his self-image and understanding of his own identity. As parents and caregivers, it is essential to provide guidance, support, and open conversations that challenge these stereotypes, allowing our boys to embrace their unique qualities and express themselves authentically.

When we explore gender considerations, our intention is not to create division or place one gender above the other. Rather, it is about gaining understanding and respect for the unique characteristics, strengths, and challenges that each gender may experience. By appreciating and acknowledging these differences, we create an environment where both sides have the opportunity to flourish and contribute in their own ways. This understanding paves the way for greater harmony and cooperation between genders, fostering a more inclusive and balanced society. It is through embracing the diversity and complementarity of genders that we can create a more harmonious and thriving world for all.

Gender-specific considerations during this period play a significant role in understanding and nurturing your growing boy. Increasing your awareness provides an opportunity to support your son's perceptions and understanding of what it means to be a boy. Here are a few areas to consider:

**Challenge Expectations:** Your son's behavior may not always align with societal stereotypes or your preconceived notions of what a boy should be like. He may exhibit emotional sensitivity, empathy, and gentleness, challenging traditional ideas of masculinity. Embrace and celebrate his individuality, appreciating the rich spectrum of emotions that boys can experience. Nurture your son's inner emotional world to help him embrace the diverse experiences and expressions of being a boy.

**Energetic Exploration:** Little boys often have an abundance of physical energy that drives their need for active play and exploration. They require ample space to move, explore their surroundings, and engage in physical activities. Recognize the importance of providing opportunities for your son to satisfy his natural curiosity and develop his physical skills.

**Gender-specific:Perceptions:** Recognizing and addressing the mixed messages and differing expectations between girls and boys is crucial as it reveals the presence of unconscious gender bias. It is important to sensitively navigate these situations and help your son understand that societal expectations and stereotypes can influence perceptions of emotions and behavior. By promoting open conversations, empathy, and critical thinking, you can help him develop a nuanced understanding of gender bias and empower him to challenge these limitations.

**Secure Emotional World:** Create a nurturing environment where your son feels understood, loved, and secure in expressing his emotions. Encourage discussions about feelings, provide opportunities for him to identify and name emotions, and validate his experiences. By fostering emotional growth, you equip your son with invaluable tools to navigate the complexities of his emotional world.

As a parent who is aware of the Boy Code and the presence of gender bias, you have a powerful role in helping your son navigate societal expectations and embrace his authentic self. Through your intentional parenting, you empower him to challenge stereotypes, cultivate emotional intelligence, and confidently navigate the world with authenticity and resilience.

## Gender Differences With Sight

At birth, there are subtle differences in sight and the eyes between boys and girls. Research suggests that female infants tend to have slightly better visual acuity, which refers to the ability to see fine details, compared to male infants.

On the other hand, male infants generally have a greater sensitivity to motion and are more responsive to visual stimuli that involve movement.

These disparities are thought to arise from both biological and neurological factors. For instance, differences in hormone levels, such as testosterone, may influence the development of visual processing systems in the brain, which can contribute to variations in visual perception between genders.

Additionally, studies have found that girls may have a slight advantage in terms of color discrimination, while boys may exhibit a higher prevalence of colorblindness. These differences can be attributed to variances in the number and distribution of color-sensitive cells in the retina.

## How do these differences play out in real life?

There is a common observation that little girls tend to gravitate towards warm colors and depict static objects, while little boys often favor cool colors and depict action-filled scenes. It is unfortunate that societal biases often lead us to praise and appreciate the more recognizable and representative drawings of little girls, such as a home, family, or pets, while overlooking the seemingly chaotic and abstract scribbles of little boys.

However, if we take the time to engage with the little boy and ask him to describe his artwork, we may be amazed by the incredibly imaginative and vibrant story he weaves. Boys often infuse their drawings with a sense of action, movement, and excitement, allowing their creativity to shine through in the form of dynamic narratives.

It is essential to recognize and embrace these inherent differences in artistic expression between boys and girls. By appreciating the unique ways in which boys and girls approach drawing, we encourage their individuality and support the development of their creative skills. Both styles of drawing are valuable and contribute to the rich tapestry of artistic expression.

## Gender Differences With Hearing

Research has indicated that there are some differences in hearing abilities between males and females. From birth, girls often possess a more advanced sense of hearing, particularly in higher frequencies associated with human speech. This disparity is attributed to the accelerated development of the inner ear structures responsible for sound processing in girls compared to boys.

The implications of these differences in hearing can affect boys' comprehension and communication skills, particularly when it comes to perceiving speech spoken by women. Boys may struggle to fully grasp and understand what is being said, leading to potential misunderstandings and communication difficulties. Unfortunately, this can result in parents and caregivers mistakenly assuming that the boy is purposefully disregarding their words when, in reality, he may have simply not heard them clearly.

To address this challenge, it is beneficial to check in with the child to ensure they have heard and comprehended the message. Parents and caregivers can proactively engage with young boys by asking simple questions like, "Did you hear what I said?" or

"Can you repeat it back to me?" This practice confirms their understanding and provides an opportunity for clarification if needed. By promoting effective communication strategies, we can minimize frustration and misunderstandings, fostering healthy communication and stronger connections between parents and young boys.

## Gender Differences With Connection

Societal pressures often place expectations on boys to separate from their mothers at an early age, promoting independence and self-reliance. This pressure stems from the Boy Code. These expectations encourage boys to be tough, independent, and emotionally reserved. Deviating from these norms can subject boys to ridicule and social exclusion, creating a challenging environment for both the child and their parents.

In response to these pressures, some parents may feel compelled to encourage their sons to separate from their mothers at an early age, fearing that their attachment might be seen as a sign of weakness or femininity. However, research indicates that the opposite is true. Boys who maintain close and secure attachments to their mothers tend to experience better emotional and social outcomes in the long run.

Instead of promoting separation, parents can focus on cultivating strong and supportive connections with their sons from the very beginning. Building a foundation of trust, emotional security, and resilience can greatly benefit boys throughout their lives. By rejecting societal expectations that discourage emotional connection, parents can provide a nurturing environment that fosters healthy social and emotional development for their sons.

## Gender Differences With Discipline

Parents often exhibit different tendencies in their disciplinary approaches, with mothers often favoring a warm and nurturing style that resonates well with little girls, while fathers tend to lean towards a firmer and more structured approach that can be effective for little boys.

The problem arises when parents try to apply a one-size-fits-all approach to discipline, based solely on their own natural tendencies, without considering the unique needs and personality of their child. This can lead to conflict and frustration, as the child may not respond well to a style that doesn't match their needs.

To avoid this, it's important for parents to become aware of their own discipline style, and to assess whether it's working well for their child. By being sensitive to their child's individual needs and preferences, parents can establish a stronger bond with their child, and help them develop the social and emotional skills they need to thrive in the world.

In general, boys tend to respond well to discipline that is firm, fair, and consistent. They often thrive in an environment where clear boundaries and expectations are set. Boys benefit from discipline that provides them with a sense of structure and guidance, helping them understand the consequences of their actions.

When it comes to communicating with boys about discipline, brevity and clarity are key. Boys tend to respond more effectively to concise instructions and explanations. Keeping the conversation focused and to the point helps them grasp the expectations and the reasoning behind the discipline.

And remember, consistency is vital for boys. When rules and consequences remain consistent, it enables them to understand and internalize behavioral expectations. Boys feel more secure and confident when they can anticipate the outcomes of their actions, fostering a sense of accountability and responsibility.

Ultimately, effective discipline involves a balance of setting appropriate boundaries, providing guidance, and fostering open communication and understanding. By recognizing and respecting individual differences while considering the broader gender tendencies, parents can create a supportive and nurturing disciplinary approach for their children.

## *Top Tips for Raising Your Boy*

**Reflect on Your Gender Biases:** Take a deep dive into your own beliefs and biases surrounding gender. Become aware of any unconscious or conscious biases you may have and strive to challenge and overcome them. It was that fishing trip when our son was three that opened my eyes to my own unconscious gender biases. This book provides you with the opportunity to begin to explore what that means for you. This can be the starting point of everything, so take some time to explore it deeply.

**Be Mindful of the Environment:** Pay attention to the messages and influences that your son encounters as he grows up. Be conscious of media, music, games, and books that may perpetuate stereotypes or present limited gender roles. Take time to identify and discuss these with your son as they arise in his environment.

**Observe Interactions:** Watch closely how adults interact with children and notice any differences that arise based on the child's gender. Identify situations where gender expectations and stereotypes may come into play. Use these situations as opportunities to enhance your own awareness and to help your son in understanding how people react and respond to him based on his gender.

**Have Open Conversations**: As your son becomes aware of societal expectations associated with the "Boy Code," engage in open and honest discussions about these situations. Let him know that he doesn't have to conform to these expectations and reassure him of your support in embracing his authentic self. This can be as simple as supporting his choice of wearing pink, for instance, when someone suggests it's a color only for girls. Take the opportunity to explain the reason behind such stereotypes and foster a sense of understanding.

**Be an Advocate**: Stand up for your son when others try to box him into the limitations of the Boy Code. Call out and raise awareness about the harmful effects of gender stereotypes. Share your knowledge and discoveries with those closest to your son, such as family, friends, and teachers.

**Learn about Gender Differences:** Educate yourself about the subtle gender differences that can significantly impact your parenting and your son's world. Understand how these differences can shape his experiences and help you navigate his development.

**Provide Love and Nurturing:** Resist the pressure to push your son away in an attempt to make him stronger or less vulnerable. Embrace the importance of providing a nurturing environment where he feels loved and supported as he grows into his own identity.

**Physical Outlets**: Recognize that your son needs physical outlets for his abundant energy. Encourage active play, sports, and other physical activities that allow him to release his energy in a healthy way.

**Literacy and Emotional Vocabulary:** Build a solid foundation in literacy and emotional vocabulary by creating an environment that promotes discussions, reading, and games centered around these aspects. Help him develop language skills to express his emotions effectively.

**Assume Positive Intentions:** Approach your son with the belief that he is always doing his best with the understanding and tools he has at that moment. If he is struggling, view it as a signal that something may be challenging for him, and support him in finding solutions.

**Create a Positive Outlook:** Take time to ensure that your son understands and feels that life is good and that he is deeply loved.

Cultivate a positive outlook, reinforce positive experiences, and celebrate his strengths and achievements.

**Discipline as Guidance**: Use discipline as a strategy to guide your son's behavior, not punish. Help him understand the impact of his actions on others and engage him in critical thinking about social situations. Encourage him to actively participate in problem-solving and finding solutions to challenges.

It is during this stage that we help our children in understanding the rules of life. Every second of every day, we have an opportunity to help them understand what it means to be kind, compassionate, honest and caring, and that we need to take care of ourselves and each other.

When they do something that is counter to your family rules, recognize that they are still very much in a stage of learning. Rather than punish the behaviour, validate the intense emotions they felt and then show them how to make amends.

For example, if they hurt a friend, after telling them you understand they were very angry when their friend took their toy, also explain that it is not ok to hurt someone. Suggest some ways to make the other child feel better (over time they will become more capable of doing this themselves). Ask them to consider if their friend would feel better if they hugged them, or if the other child is crying, suggest taking a tissue over to wipe away the tears.

Our children do not need to be punished. They need to know we love them, even when they misbehave. However, it's important to emphasize that there are 'rules of conduct' that we all follow to create a peaceful world. They need to take responsibility for their actions, and work toward finding a solution to the situation.

Remember, every child is unique, and these tips can serve as a general guide. Adapt them to fit your son's individual needs, personality, and development. Stay attuned to his growth and environment, provide unconditional love and support, and enjoy the journey of raising your remarkable boy into becoming a remarkable man.

## *Summary*

Raising boys involves understanding and navigating various gender-specific considerations throughout their development.

Boys may experience differences in language development making it important for parents to provide a literacy-rich environment, engage in meaningful conversations, and encourage language development through storytelling and reading.

Boys may encounter societal messages and expectations that shape their emotional perception. The Boy Code and gender stereotypes may discourage boys from expressing emotions or seeking emotional support. Parents can create a safe space for boys to explore and express their emotions, fostering emotional intelligence and empathy.

The Boy Code may encourage boys to distance themselves from their mothers, suppress emotions, or adopt specific behaviors associated with masculinity. It is crucial for parents to challenge harmful stereotypes, embrace their son's unique qualities, and foster a sense of authenticity and self-acceptance.

Boys thrive in a nurturing and supportive environment. Parents can provide love, affection, and emotional support, resisting the urge to push boys towards independence prematurely. Creating opportunities for physical outlets and promoting healthy outlets for their energy can also contribute to their overall well-being.

Boys benefit from firm, fair, and consistent discipline that provides clear boundaries and expectations. Parents should adopt a style that balances structure and guidance with understanding and empathy, ensuring that discipline strategies are tailored to their individual needs.

By being aware of these gender-specific considerations and actively addressing them, parents can help boys develop their full potential, navigate societal expectations, and cultivate a strong sense of self. It is through understanding, empathy, and intentional parenting that boys can flourish and grow into confident, compassionate individuals – remarkable men.

## *The Top 3 Questions Parents Ask*

*1. My best friend's daughter was born a few weeks before my son and we have been raising them together. Now that they are toddlers there have been times when we have watched a Disney movie together. My friend's daughter can watch it all the way through, but my son often gets frightened by certain parts and needs some comfort with me to regain control of his emotions. I'm worried if his sensitivity is something I should be concerned about and if he will outgrow it?*

Your son's sensitivity is a beautiful quality that should be celebrated and nurtured. In a society that often pressures boys to conform to certain masculine stereotypes (the Boy Code), it's important to create a safe and supportive environment at home where he feels comfortable expressing all of his emotions. When he feels scared or sad while watching a movie, provide him with the support and comfort he needs to navigate those big feelings. Let him know that his emotions are valid and that it's okay to express them.

If you sense that he may feel embarrassed because his female friend isn't as affected by certain scenes in the movie, use this as an opportunity to teach him about the diversity of emotional experiences. Explain that everyone processes emotions differently, and it's perfectly okay for him to have his own unique responses. Emphasize how empathetic he is to the characters and highlight the beauty of his sensitivity.

Your son's ability to empathize and show compassion is a valuable trait that will serve him well throughout his life. I would worry more about the lack of sensitivity than the abundance of it. I would also hope my son never outgrew it!

*2. My son is like the unstoppable Energizer Bunny, constantly in motion He moves all the time! I find myself exhausted trying to keep up with his endless need for activity. Is this ever going to end?*

Boys are wired to move, and testosterone, a hormone predominantly found in males, plays a significant role in shaping their behavior and energy levels. Testosterone is known to contribute to increased physical activity, drive, and competitiveness in boys and men.

As boys pass through different stages of growth, the impact of testosterone on their behavior may evolve. During early childhood, boys may exhibit high levels of physical energy and a strong desire for active play. They may engage in rough-and-tumble play, enjoy running and jumping, and have an innate need for movement to release their energy.

Understanding the role of testosterone and its impact on behaviour can help parents and caregivers create an environment that supports their natural tendencies while also guiding them towards responsible and positive expressions of their energy.

Providing opportunities for movement, physical activity, and structured/unstructured play can help boys channel their energy in healthy and productive ways. It's crucial to strike a balance between encouraging their natural inclination to move and ensuring they understand appropriate behavior, boundaries, and respect for others.

Things will change over time but testosterone will always be part of the male makeup so it is good to try and understand how this affects our boys, and how we can support them. Get creative in thinking of ways to let him release his energy while not completely draining yours! And remember, this too will pass.

3. *As my son is now three, shouldn't he be less clingy to me and need me less? He seems overly attached to me. Is that normal for boys?*

Yes! It is completely normal and beneficial for a boy to have a strong attachment to his mother, especially during the early years of development. The close bond between a mother and her son provides numerous advantages that should be celebrated and nurtured.

The concern that arises regarding the intensity of this attachment often stems from the societal pressures imposed by the Boy Code. This set of expectations and stereotypes dictates that boys should be independent and self-reliant from a young age.

However, it is crucial to recognize that these expectations are not based on the individual needs and developmental stages of each child.

In reality, the strong connection between a mother and her son can have profound positive effects on his overall well-being and future development. Research has shown that boys who have a secure attachment to their mothers tend to perform better academically during their school years. They are also less likely to engage in risky behaviors during adolescence and have more fulfilling relationships as adults.

Fostering a solid attachment to their mothers contributes to boys' mental health and emotional resilience. It provides a safe and nurturing space for them to explore their own emotions, express vulnerability, and develop a strong sense of self.

To gain a different perspective, let's reframe the question: Would you be concerned if your three-year-old daughter showed a similar attachment to you?

Most likely, the answer would be no, as society often views mother-daughter attachment as more acceptable and even desirable. That dichotomy is why it is so important to challenge these biases and treat the attachment needs of boys with the same understanding and support.

As your son continues to grow and mature, he will naturally begin to explore his independence and expand his social interactions. Encouraging gradual steps towards autonomy while providing a secure base of support will help him navigate this developmental stage with confidence.

Remember, every child is unique, and their attachment needs may vary. Trust your instincts as a parent and provide the love, care, and support that your son needs to flourish. Embrace his attachment to you as a source of strength and connection that will positively shape his development and well-being.

Celebrate the special bond between you and your son, and cherish this precious time of closeness and affection. It is a foundation that will support his growth into a resilient, confident, and compassionate individual.

# The Young Years (4~8)

# *Perspectives*

## The Parents' View

These years are truly delightful, and if a strong foundation has been laid, you'll begin to have rich and meaningful conversations with your son, gaining insight into his emotional world and perspectives on life. He'll still be in the process of learning to manage his emotions, but you're unlikely to see the same frequency of tantrums and meltdowns that characterized the toddler years. His zest for life and sense of adventure will be infectious, bringing warmth to your heart. It's important to cultivate and preserve the enchantment in his world, along with a sense of safety, love, and acceptance.

This is also the time when we may feel more societal pressure to push our little boys away, prepare them for the real world, protect them from being seen as weak, or vulnerable, or a mama's boy. Once they step foot in an institutional environment their world view begins to change. From being the center of the universe with rather free reign to be as active as they need to be, to being expected to control both their impulses and their energy, little boys soon experience the reality of the educational systems. Everything starts to change.

During these years, societal pressures to conform to traditional masculine stereotypes can start to take hold, and the educational system may not always meet the needs of our little boys. This can cause them to feel frustrated, discouraged, and even ashamed of their natural inclinations. As parents, we have the power to help our sons navigate these challenges and maintain their spark for life. By listening to them, validating their emotions, and advocating for their needs, we can help them feel seen, heard, and loved for who they are.

## The Mother's View

As your son becomes more independent, you notice fewer tantrums, but when they do happen, you find yourself having less patience than you did the first time around. Explosive emotions still overtake him at times.

You begin to see subtle differences between little girls and little boys. You didn't expect your son to be so emotionally soft and tender. You're starting to notice disparities between what you thought a boy would be by now and what you're actually experiencing.

You become aware of how others treat your son and what they expect from him. It's disheartening when they fail to see the sweetness in your little guy. Some friends with daughters act like their girls need protection from your adventurous warrior (but you believe the opposite is often true!).

Challenges arise as your boy enters school. He starts with excitement, but soon he struggles to meet the expectations of this new environment. Your heart breaks as you see the spark in your little guy begin to fade.

You start questioning your own parenting and wonder if you're being overprotective. Should you push him to conform to what society expects, even if it's not his true self?

Listening to other moms talk about their boys sometimes leaves you feeling disconnected. You know your son is sweet, sensitive, and empathetic, but it seems like the world isn't always supporting these traits. You're determined to find ways to help your little guy thrive, no matter what it takes. Your Mother Bear side may start to come out.

## The Father's View

This age is resonating with you. You've gained more confidence in your parenting skills, making it easier to relate to your growing son compared to his baby years. It warms your heart to see him imitating you and adopting your style. You feel more involved and recognize your importance as part of the parenting team, and you're starting to have fun!

Having deep conversations with your son is a new and rewarding experience. Now that he can express himself, you get glimpses into his thoughts and emotions, allowing for more meaningful connections.

Your son's emotional world becomes more intricate during these years. He may experience a wider range of emotions and may need your support and guidance in managing and understanding his feelings. It can be challenging to find the right words to say and strike a balance between what he needs to hear and what you want to convey.

With increased independence, your son may test boundaries and exhibit challenging behaviors. This can lead to moments of frustration and reflection as you figure out effective discipline strategies while fostering a loving and respectful relationship.

You are increasingly aware of your crucial role in shaping your son's understanding of masculinity. Supporting a positive and healthy perspective of what it means to be male is essential as he looks up to you as a role model, learning from your actions and words. Your influence as a positive male figure in his life is becoming more significant than ever before.

## The Son's View

Your son is among the group of kindergarten children who are gathered around tables, quietly working on an activity. It is a quiet and calm classroom scene - until the recess bell rings. Then there is an explosion of activity. The boys, including your son, bolt out of the door almost before the last sound of that bell, racing out into the playground. They are playing some kind of running tag game, having a grand time, and everyone seems to understand what the rules are. Your boy is a frenzy of activity. It is simply a wildness of movement that doesn't stop until the bell rings again to signal recess is over. It's been 20 minutes. The boys never stopped moving. Slowly, painstakingly they return to their class, seemingly savoring every extra second outside. That 20 minutes has to satisfy their body's need to move for the next two hours. Your son looks a little downhearted as he walks quietly in line, back to the classroom.

Excitement and confusion predominate his world. He starts to 'get in trouble' at school more often and struggles with understanding the expectations and then being able to comply. His world has suddenly gone off kilter and he needs his family world to keep him balanced and feeling loved and secure.

## *The Early Schooling Years*

It used to be that these years, before the start of formal schooling, were a time when boys fulfilled their need to be warriors and hunters in the safe, creative world of their backyards. Formal schooling was still off in the horizon and the child was still the center of his world. What in the world has happened? And how is this impacting our fearless young leaders?

## Changes

During the years between 4 and 8 boys lose some of their little boyishness and start to become young boys. Milestones such as starting a big school, losing a tooth, joining a sports club or music lessons, and developing more friendships often highlight the stage.

During the early years of Kindergarten and lower elementary school, there may be some warning signs that our young boys are struggling. Initially, they may be filled with eagerness and excitement to attend school like the older children and participate in more 'big boy' activities. However, over time, that enthusiasm may begin to dwindle, and they may start to express reluctance to go to school or exhibit signs of stress.

By the end of first grade, many boys have learned how to conform, mask their true selves and emotions, and navigate an academic environment that does not cater to their unique learning needs. They may struggle to keep up with the pace of instruction, or they may find it difficult to sit still and focus for long periods, which can lead to further feelings of frustration and inadequacy.

It is essential to recognize signals of distress and take action to support our boys. Parents can work with teachers and school administrators to ensure that the environment their son is spending a great part of his day in, is one where he feels confident and successful. It can be an environment where his need for movement is catered to and projects are a way of reaching curricular standards.

By providing a safe and supportive environment where boys and girls can learn and grow in their own unique way, we can help them develop the confidence and resilience they need to succeed both academically and personally.

Boys can sometimes lag behind girls by as much as two years, and the educational system often favors the learning styles and preferences of young girls. This is a well-known fact. Boys may hear too often that they are not performing well, that they need to focus better, or that they should be more like their female peers. These negative messages can deal a severe blow to their self-esteem.

## The Fall Out That Comes Home After School

The pressure from early academic demands adds to the discord in your young boy's life. In the past, formal education often started around 6 years old, but now, many children begin some form of care outside the home as early as 3 years old. The academic bar has been set much higher, and the expectations for our young boys might not align with their developmental stage.

As a result, the pressure to perform and conform can lead to rebellion, misbehavior, and damage to their self-esteem. What your little boy truly needs is a home that serves as a sanctuary—a place where he can recharge, feel accepted, and loved unconditionally.

I remember so vividly my sweet little Kindergarten boy coming home every Friday crestfallen and disappointed. All week long he would strive to do his best in hopes of earning the coveted title of 'Star of The Week'. Almost every week, that recognition went to one of the girls. He tried so hard to listen to the teacher, to do all that was asked of him, to sit still when he was supposed to, to write out his letters and numbers when he was directed to. But despite all of his efforts, it took months before he was named a Star. This experience broke my heart, and ignited an anger at a system that didn't cherish our boys and allow them to thrive. Instead we have pushed them into an unnatural category that has made success challenging and undermined their unique potential.

Parents truly have the power to be partners in education, going beyond just a catchphrase. By collaborating with schools, we can work together to create an environment that also works for our boys and ensure they have meaningful and enjoyable experiences in their educational journey. While schools focus on the big picture, we, as parents, zoom in on our son's individual portrait and how it fits into the larger canvas. Our focused drive can be a potent force for positive change. Both views are necessary to create that change.

To make a meaningful impact, it's essential to do our research and approach teachers and school leaders with well-informed perspectives rather than purely emotional reactions. Sharing information and proposing new best practices can open avenues for discussion and progress. Volunteering to support change can also demonstrate our dedication and influence.

When delving into possible improvements, consider these ideas to kickstart your efforts:

❖ Have a later entry start time for boys. Starting at least one year later than girls can profoundly impact their educational experience.

❖ Understand the differences in learning styles and provide more hands-on project learning.

❖ Provide time and space for creative exploration and play.

❖ Incorporate movement breaks throughout the day. Utilize activities like games, outdoor exploration, and structured physical exercises to keep them engaged and focused.

❖ Provide male role models in the classroom environment.

❖ Consider flexible assessments to accommodate different learning styles. For instance, a female kindergarten teacher asks the children to draw a picture of their family to assess their understanding of the current unit of study. In this scenario, the little girls create vibrant, detailed drawings including family members, homes and elements of nature. The teacher ranks these as being demonstrations of comprehension. The boys present abstract drawings full of lines and circles, which seem like chaotic scribbles to the teacher. She assumes the boys did not understand the unit they explored. However, if she had understood about gender differences, she would have involved the boys in verbally narrating the story behind their drawing. That would have been the evidence the teacher was looking for. The boys understood very well but expressed it very differently from the girls.

The list goes on and on. This is simply a place to start.

# *Reflections from the Frontlines*

There is an unparalleled purity and innocence found in young children that distinguishes them from any other stage of development. Their experiences are the raw data they are using to compile their understanding of the world around them. They resemble the most advanced forms of AI in how they absorb and sort each and every aspect of the world they occupy. They are simply amazing. Their curiosity and sense of wonder are boundless, and they approach the world with unfiltered enthusiasm. They remind us to appreciate the beauty in the simplest of things and find joy in the everyday wonders we may have long taken for granted.

Even before having my own son, as a teacher of young children, I discovered a captivating beauty in my interactions with the young boys in my classroom. I loved their raw energy, their intense emotions, their curiosity and unwavering determination to tackle challenges. They absolutely vibrated with energy when they could somehow give assistance and help someone.

It wasn't that I was some kind of a super teacher, but the boys in my care flourished and felt a profound sense of respect and love.

Problems were minimal. That was not the case for many of my colleagues over the years.

Although in those early years of my career I had not yet begun the deep dive into the world of boys, I intuitively understood that their needs were different. Boys especially responded well to my style that some people might have coined as being too strict. I had high expectations for behaviour, regardless of gender, and I was fair, firm and very consistent. Once the classroom environment was established, a very safe and secure space lent to great learning experiences for us all.

It was hard work and took a lot of energy, just like parenting does, but the results were more than worth the effort.

Painting a picture of doom and gloom regarding our young boys and their education is all too easy. Throughout my extensive experience working with children and their parents, I have witnessed the dedication of teachers who tirelessly strive to create enriching learning experiences.

These educators go above and beyond to craft engaging projects, find innovative ways to cover curriculum standards, and keep the students excited about learning. They recognize the significance of involving parents as partners in their child's educational journey, maintaining open lines of communication.

Teaching is a labor of love, as most educators don't enter the profession for financial gain or public recognition. Instead, their passion lies in working with children and having a positive impact on their lives.

Nonetheless, teachers often face constraints within the educational system they work in, making it challenging to bring about significant changes on their own. But when parents become active supporters of their child's education, positive transformations can occur. By fostering a strong partnership between parents and teachers, we can create an environment that truly nurtures our little boys' educational journeys. Together, we can ensure that our boys receive the best possible support and encouragement to thrive academically and emotionally.

## *Reflections from a Kindergarten Teacher*

For some children, this marks their initial exposure to formal education. The classrooms are inviting, often arranged with diverse activity centers throughout the space, with a large carpet in the center for class meetings. A comfy corner equipped with books and cushions offers a place for children to unwind with a story. Typically, there's a block corner with an array of blocks for imaginative construction. An art station, a science area, a writing nook, and a zone for hands-on activities and puzzles complete the kindergarten setting.

Children enjoy some autonomy in their choices while the teacher strives to cultivate an environment conducive to social learning and exploration. As the school year begins, children experience a blend of enthusiasm, excitement and apprehension. Teachers, typically women, have a strong passion for their work and genuinely enjoy engaging with children.

A curriculum must be covered, and skilled teachers can largely integrate standards into projects with some intentional planning. Challenges can arise, especially for young boys, when expectations aren't aligned with their developmental capacities. Writing letters and numbers can be tough for little boys who may not have developed fine motor skills yet. Their social skills often trail behind those of girls by about a year or more, making it more difficult for them to sit still and concentrate for extended periods. Additionally, young boys frequently exude high levels of energy, which can present a considerable task for kindergarten teachers.

Little boys have to work really hard to stay out of trouble in Kindergarten. They are wired to move, to use their whole body and have a great need to feel competent and capable. They love to explore, create, build and solve problems.

The more a kindergarten program can cater to the needs of both little boys and girls, the richer the overall experience becomes. When there is more emphasis on social/emotional learning rather than academic pursuits, Kindergarten can be a place where all the students have a chance to feel success.

## *Reflections from a Grade 1 Teacher*

This is where elementary school begins. As the school bell rings and the academic journey continues, Grade 1 marks a significant milestone for both teachers and their young students.

The classroom environment is very different from the year before. Desks and tables take up more space, and the playfulness of a Kindergarten space is much less evident. School feels a bit more serious - especially for the little boys, often causing both excitement and apprehension.

One of the main challenges teachers face is helping boys in the class to stay focused and on task. They often become easily distracted, which can hinder their academic progress. Some boys struggle to work collaboratively with their peers, and this affects how actively they can engage in the group activities.

Boys can start to fall behind - behind the girls that is. Misbehavior can be a signal that something is not right in their emotional world. Boys crave positive connections with their teachers and peers. When they feel respected, understood, and valued, school life is a more positive experience.

The young boy who has explosive outbursts for apparently no reason may actually be feeling overwhelmed and disconnected. Rather than being given a Time Out, he benefits from the teacher giving calm guidance, comfort and understanding.

The young boy who has numerous meltdowns throughout the day might be really frustrated and angry that he can't seem to do what his classmates are doing. He needs his teacher to be patient and understanding, helping him feel more connected and successful.

Grade 1 is a critical stage of learning and perhaps more geared for our boys when they are a year or two older.

## *Reflections from a Grade 2 Teacher*

The academic demands have increased and too many boys are starting to really fall behind, while many of the girls seem to thrive and excel in the face of new challenges. Sometimes, the girls, fueled by their own successes, occasionally make fun of their less competent male classmates. As a result, some boys may respond with rebellion and outbursts, while others may withdraw and shut down emotionally. It's crucial for teachers to be sensitive to these dynamics and create a supportive and inclusive classroom environment.

By this stage expectations for both behavior and academic competence are high. Teachers feel pressured to meet curricular requirements and class time may have an emphasis on the skills and knowledge acquisition. It becomes evident that there is a wide range of academic readiness, and in general, boys may be showing signs of struggle. This situation can lead to more frustration and disengagement.

This is also a time when some boys begin to have challenges around time management and organizational skills. They forget to complete assignments or misplace important materials, impacting their overall academic performance.

For many young boys, this year can be particularly challenging. The natural love for learning and curiosity they once had may start to fade as they internalize negative perceptions of themselves. As teachers and parents, it's essential to uplift and encourage our boys, providing them with the support they need to embrace their unique strengths and navigate the challenges they encounter along the way. By nurturing their confidence and sense of self-worth, we can help them regain their enthusiasm for learning and life.

# *Behaviour*

*Johnny steps off the school bus to where his mother is eagerly waiting for him. With a warm smile, she asks about his day.
He throws down his backpack and shouts at the top of his lungs, 'I hate school! And I hate you!'*

*Johnny, who is transitioning into an academic kindergarten class with 20 other students, half of them girls, has been struggling with self-regulation and following the rules. He has been in Time Out twice already, and feels his teacher favors the girls over him.*

*Despite understanding the importance of Johnny adjusting and integrating into the class, his mother's heart aches to see him so miserable. She doesn't understand why it is so hard for him.*

Pre-K and Kindergarten are typically the first formal education experiences for many young boys. It can be a harsh awakening to realize that you can't just:

❖ move around every time you feel like it
❖ go outside and do what you want to do for as long as you want to do it

❖ be yourself; you need to be able to regulate your behaviour
❖ do anything as good as the girls in class can.

Around the age of 4, according to experts like Steven Biddulph, some boys experience a natural surge of hormones which can cause an increase in their physical activity and need for movement. This can make it challenging for them to sit still and concentrate in structured settings like a classroom, which often has strict rules and expectations for behavior. As a result, their behavior may change and become more disruptive or energetic, which can be challenging for all involved.

During this stage, boys require more freedom to move, ample space to explore and play, and numerous opportunities to be creative and adventurous. They also need moments of autonomy where they can make their own choices. Unfortunately, this is the same time when they are expected to remain calm, still, and quiet for most of the school day. It's a challenging dichotomy for these young boys to navigate, and it can lead to feelings of frustration, inadequacy, and confusion.

Between the ages of 4 and 8, boys experience important changes that influence how they act and interact with the world. One common trait seen in many boys at this time is their boundless energy. They love activities that involve running, jumping, and physical play. Their curiosity drives them to explore and learn about their surroundings through hands-on experiences.

Boys in this stage are playful and imaginative. They enjoy pretending and making up games using action figures, building blocks, and imaginary worlds. However, their impulsiveness can sometimes lead to risky behavior and accidents as they act without thinking through the consequences.

Socially, boys are forming deeper friendships and learning how to navigate social situations. They practice sharing, cooperation, and taking turns, even though conflicts with friends can arise.

As they grow, boys crave more independence and want to make decisions on their own. This can sometimes cause clashes with adults, especially when their desires differ from expectations.

Every child is unique, influenced by their own personalities, surroundings, and experiences.

## Mis-Behaviour

When our little boys misbehave, it's an opportunity for us to guide them with solid and supportive guidance. Remember, they are still learning about life and how they fit into the world.

Misbehavior is a signal that your son is giving you that something is wrong in his emotional world. When his inner world is in turmoil or conflict, often his behavior will reflect that with aggressiveness or outbursts. He is trying to tell you something is wrong but can't communicate that with you.

As a parent we sometimes react to the behaviour with disciplinary measures. Your son has a complete meltdown when you ask him to put away his game for dinner. You can't reason with him. The meltdown intensifies. Finally, you tell him to go to his room until he is calm enough to talk to you.

So, what might have been behind that behavior? It probably is not about that game!

He might have had a really hard day at school with one bad thing happening after another. When you tell him to put his game away, it is just the last straw. He can't take anything more.

Or he knows that his parents are going out tonight and a new babysitter is coming after supper. Your son is quite worried about someone new coming, and both his parents leaving. When you tell him to put the game away he knows the time that you will be leaving and the babysitter comes is getting closer. He is very anxious. He has a meltdown.

When we can look past the behavior long enough to get to the real problem, the emotion that is driving the behavior, then we have a good chance of being able to support our sons better.

Imagine if behind those tantrums, outbursts, and meltdowns, your son is actually experiencing emotions like sadness, fear, anxiety, frustration, disappointment, or disconnection. If we could glimpse the real emotions driving their behavior, would we respond the same? Would we still feel the need to punish them?

Misbehavior is often a signal—a cry for help, a call for connection. Rather than solely focusing on the outward behavior, it's crucial to delve deeper and understand what's truly behind it. This is where the path to genuine connection begins.

When your child is angry or upset, your primary goal should be to restore a sense of safety, which requires your calm and supportive presence. Instead of resorting to "time-outs" that might leave children feeling isolated with their overwhelming feelings, try a "time-in" approach. Stay with your child and help them navigate through their emotions. You'll be amazed at how much self-control they can develop when they feel less alone and more supported. A simple "I'm right here... You're safe... I'm listening" can work wonders.

A child's misbehavior sometimes arises when their fundamental needs are not met, as depicted in Maslow's hierarchy of needs. Factors like lack of sleep, stress hormones flooding their brain, or low blood sugar may be at play. Punishments that threaten their sense of safety and belonging can exacerbate the situation.

Acting out is a cry for help, a cry for love. When we respond to poor behavior with anger or punishment, it distances us and invalidates the child's feelings, often sending them deeper into the feeling that caused the poor behavior in the first place. Contrary to the myth, not punishing children won't spoil them. Instead, it fosters emotional intelligence, helps them process their emotions, and strengthens their trust in us.

The goal is to teach them to articulate their feelings instead of acting them out. When children feel heard, validated and understood, they are less likely to resort to misbehavior. By creating a safe and empathetic environment, we sow the seeds for emotional growth and lasting connections.

## Discipline

Discipline can become a significant challenge for both parents and teachers at this time. This period can be overwhelming and confusing for your boys as they transition from the comfort and safety of home to an educational system not always designed to cater to their unique needs. It is essential to recognize that little boys may be up to two years behind in certain developmental areas compared to girls, and the educational system often favors learning styles more common among girls. Little boys in pre-kindergarten, kindergarten, and first grade may not be as socially or emotionally advanced as their female peers.

An overwhelming majority of teachers in these early grades are women, which can make it challenging for little boys who may have different ways of communicating and learning. For a little boy who is full of energy and excitement, being confined to a classroom for most of the day can be frustrating and discouraging. They may struggle to adjust to being in a group, having to sit still for long periods of time, and learning in a way that doesn't come naturally to them.

Given these challenges, it's understandable that little boys may feel like they are constantly getting in trouble or not fitting in at school. It's important that we provide them with support and guidance as they navigate this period of their lives. Rather than focusing solely on discipline, it's important to take a holistic approach that recognizes their unique needs and strengths. This may include providing them with opportunities to be more active and creative, encouraging their curiosity and sense of wonder, and helping them to develop social and emotional skills that will serve them well in school and beyond. By recognizing and valuing what makes little boys special, we can help them to thrive and succeed in the classroom and beyond.

It's good to remember that 'a child is always doing the best that they are capable of' in that particular moment. If the child is not capable of certain behavior then it's unrealistic for us to be expecting that. While the educational system is gradually changing to better accommodate diverse learning styles, as parents, we play a significant role in helping our boys during this transitional period.

When you get messages from the teacher that your boy is acting out or there was this problem or that problem or the other problem, and she sends homework for him to do that is going to take an hour to complete, you're going to have to make some decisions yourself.

In any decisions that you make, always prioritize your relationship with your son. Let him know there is nothing wrong with him; instead the system may not always cater to his unique qualities as a male. Take special care in those times after school, on weekends, and on holidays to reignite that spark he may be starting to lose.

In a world that may seem not to fully appreciate their unique qualities, you can be a source of unwavering support, letting your little boy know that they are valued and loved just as they are. By fostering a strong and supportive home environment, you can empower your son to tackle the challenges of the educational system with confidence and determination.

# Discipline and Dialogue

Frequently, punishment and discipline follow instances of misbehavior. There's a common belief that without punishment, children won't grasp the necessary lesson, potentially leading to persistent issues. But just how impactful is this approach, and what possible alternatives are there?

What's wrong with punishment? Remember that misbehavior is a signal that something is not right in your child's world. Already grappling with internal distress, imposing punishment can inadvertently dismiss their need for connection, leaving them feeling misunderstood and unsupported. Such a response might trigger them to vent more anger, even to the point of expressing hatred. Or, they might have thoughts of revenge, leading to increased defiance. Worst of all, they may internalize a sense of shame, perceiving themselves as undeserving of your affection, leading to self-pity and plummeting self-esteem.

Punishment severs the connection between you and your child. It often prioritizes control over intimacy. While we can enforce actions, we cannot dictate their emotions. And that is what is wrong with punishment - we risk damaging the emotional landscape between us and our children.

There are alternatives that work even more effectively, still holding your son accountable for the misbehavior. Just find the right one for your child and you.

## Alternatives to Discipline:

❖ **Point to a way he can be helpful.** For instance, imagine you're driving home from preschool with your two young children in the back seat. A disagreement between them, resulting in tears due to the actions of your son. You have to step in, express disapproval and firmly remind him of what the expectations are for behaviour. Emotions are running high. You suggest he passes his sibling a tissue to help rectify the situation. He likely feels remorse for the situation and might want to mend things. To reopen communication and reconnect, consider asking for his help in the store, "Could you go and choose two big oranges for us?" This shifts the focus away from the initial conflict, allowing both of you to move forward without lingering tension. It's a fresh start where no negativity is being carried forward.

❖ **Express strong disapproval** (without attacking) It's perfectly fine to show your feelings - in fact it is good role modeling. It helps your son connect the action he did with the feeling you have. For instance, you could say, "I'm furious you are walking in dirty shoes on the freshly scrubbed floor." After stating your disapproval, remember to create a way for him to correct the situation, "There is a rag under the sink you can use to wipe up your footprints."

❖ **State your expectations.** Make it clear what the process is - what he needs to do. For example, you could say, "I expect my stapler returned to my desk after you're done." Often miscommunication occurs when what we say and what our boys hear are not the same. The clearer we are, the more likely it is to achieve the desired outcome. It can be helpful to have him repeat back to you what the expectation you just stated was.

❖ **Guide your child in how to make amends.** Offer a way for him to take a positive step towards repairing the situation. Since there has been a disconnect, you might suggest a concrete action he can take. For example, if your son has hurt another child in anger, after prioritizing safety, encourage your son to inquire directly with the injured child about ways to make amends. This might include offering a heartfelt apology, providing a comforting gesture like a hug, or actively participating in fixing any damage caused. This approach not only fosters accountability on your child's part but also has him taking responsibility to improve the situation he caused.

❖ **Offer a choice.** This lets him feel he has some control of the situation, some power, within certain boundaries. "No running. You can either walk by my side or sit in the trolley." This gives him the ability to decide while still adhering to the stipulated options. This strategy works well at all ages. It allows you as the parent to set the boundaries, but also empowers your child to make his own choices.

❖ **You can take decisive action** when misbehavior is linked to a specific item. Gently and calmly you can remove the item and state, "It seems to be too difficult to do this right now so I am putting it away. We can try again another time." This communicates that the behaviour led to a consequence, while also leaving room for a future opportunity.

❖ **Allow your child to experience the consequences of his/her misbehavior.** "You didn't eat above the table, now you have to sweep the floor. You need to clean up your mess." This teaches responsibility and accountability for his behaviour.

## Timed Silence

Timed Silence, a term first coined by Dr. William Pollack, refers to the period of time during which many boys require to process an emotionally challenging experience before being able to discuss it. It is the space they need to move from the negative emotions of the experience and reach a point where they can openly talk about it.

Before I learned about this concept, I often made the same mistake many women do. I assumed communication styles between males and females were the same. At the beginning of my marriage, there were times of conflict where my responses did more to disrupt our connection rather than deepen it. In the throes of intense emotions, I insisted that we face the conflict head-on, immediately, and hash it out until we came to some kind of an understanding. I wanted to take action as soon as that first spark of conflict ignited. Unfortunately, the result of this communication approach often resulted in a much larger, raging fire for a while. If I had understood about Timed Silence things might have been significantly less chaotic and turbulent in those years. Understanding the importance of allowing time between the conflict's eruption and the subsequent discussion would have helped avoid a great deal of wasted negative energy.

Every male has his own, individual clock that will determine how much time he needs to be silent before opening up to share his feelings. When, as parents, we recognize and are sensitive to our son's unique timing, we set the stage for honest conversations.

## *After An Explosion*

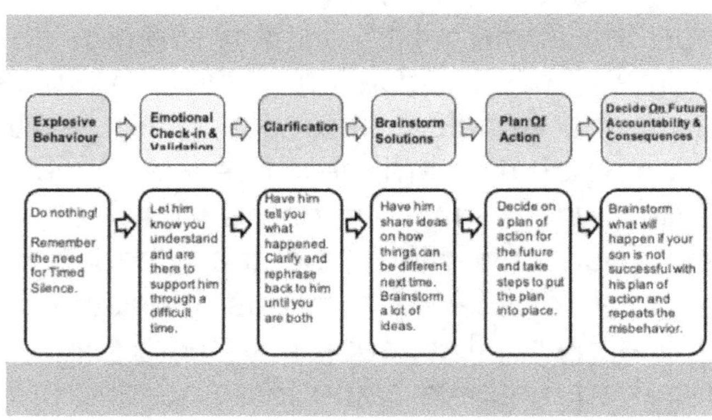


**What to do after your son has had some big feelings? Guide him!**

Let's look at a real example:

## 1. There has been an explosive incident.

Your six- year-old son, Eric, is playing soccer with his friend Brody in the backyard. Brody steals the ball away from Eric and scores a goal. Eric shouts 'FOUL! - No goal! He picks up the ball and throws it at Brody, hitting him hard in the face.

Brody starts to cry and runs towards the house yelling, 'I'm telling your mom on you.' After applying first aid to Brody's face, you suggest that play time is done for the day and it's time for Brody to go home. Eric has been fuming at the kitchen table the entire time. He is still red-faced and upset. You suggest he go have a shower. (Timed Silence).

## 2. Emotional Check-In and Validation.

When Eric returns he looks calmer. He sits at the table and you say, 'Feeling a bit better after the shower? You were really mad at Brody earlier. I could see that you were having a hard time.'

## 3. Clarification.

Now you can ask him if he is ready to talk about what happened.

You: It looked like something really upset you when you and Brody were playing soccer. Can you tell me what happened?

Eric: Brody tripped me when he stole the ball from me but he said he got a goal. He fouled me, mom!

You: So, Brody got the ball away from you and scored a goal. Brody tripped you so you felt that was a foul, so no goal.

Eric: Right! You can't get a goal if you foul someone. That's the rule! He fouled me!

You: Got it. So what happened next?

Eric: I got really mad so I threw the ball at him.

You: Hmm. You were angry because you thought he fouled you so you threw the ball at him.

Eric: Yeah.

## 4. Brainstorm Solutions

You: What do you think about the choice you made?

Eric: I didn't mean to hurt Brody and make him cry. I was really mad.

You: I get it. Not a great choice, so what are you going to do about it? How can you fix this problem with Brody?

Eric: I don't know. (and you wait - give him time to think) Maybe I could go to his house and say sorry.

You: That's an idea. Any others?

Eric: Brody really likes my card collection. I could take them over to his house and let him play with them.

You: Can you think of anything else to help make the situation better?

Eric: Maybe I could draw a picture of us playing soccer and write, I'm sorry, on it.

You: Wow. You have three good ideas there. You could go to his house and apologize. You could take over your card collection and share them with him. Or you could draw a picture of the two of you playing soccer and write you are sorry on it. Which one sounds like the best idea to you?

Eric: Hmmm. I think drawing a picture and then taking it over would make him feel the best.

You: That is a good choice. You can get started once we are done talking

## 5. Plan of Action

You: Let's think a bit about the future. Let's say Brody comes over again someday to play soccer and the very same thing, or something like it, happens. Something where you feel something unfair has happened and get really angry. How are you going to keep yourself from making the same kind of mistake? What are you going to do differently?

Eric: I don't know.

You: You have just shown that you can come up with some great solutions to problems. Let's try and come up with two or three ideas to look at. I can think of one. Maybe you could both agree on some rules to follow from the start. Can you think of something?

Eric: Maybe we could come and get you if we have a fight about if something was fair or not - like a referee.

You: Good idea. What else?

Eric: Maybe we could try and talk about it before getting so mad. Our teacher said it's good to drink some water when you feel like your brain isn't working so well. Maybe when there is a foul we stop the game and drink some water and then try and talk about it.

You: You have three good options. Which one do you want to choose to use in the future if the same kind of problem happens.

Eric: I like the water idea. My teacher says it really works well to get your brain working.

## 6. Decide on Future Accountability & Consequences

You: Great. Last thing to talk about here is, what is going to happen if a problem comes up and even though you decided to use the water idea, you get so mad that you forget and you hurt Brody again? What will be the way to handle that?

Eric: Don't worry, mom. I won't forget.

You: I know you are going to do your best. But we need to decide now on the consequences if you don't follow your plan. It is not ok to hurt someone when you lose your temper.

Eric: If I do it again, maybe Brody and I shouldn't be allowed to play soccer together for a week.

You: That sounds like a fair consequence. Let's hope we don't need to do that. I know how much you guys love playing soccer here. I know you will do your best to remember. I can help by reminding you to have your water bottles close by, too. Ok, how about you start on that picture for Brody.

Eric: Ok. Thanks, mom!

Big hug - problem solved.

When thinking about guiding your son, here are 5 things he really needs from you:

#1: **Rules**

❖ **Clear -** Expectations and boundaries need to be clearly defined. Providing clear rules and guidelines helps him feel secure and confident, as he knows what is required of him in various situations. Does he understand what behaviour is acceptable and what is not? Role play them so that it is clear. Does he understand why the rules are in place? The rules need to make sense to him. He learns that rules and consequences apply to everyone equally.

❖ **Concise** - Keep the rules straightforward and to the point. Boys might find it challenging to follow long-winded explanations or complicated instructions. Fewer words are more effective.

❖ **Fair** - Boys have a strong sense of justice, and they need rules that are fair and equitable. If a rule needs to be adjusted for a specific situation, make sure it's communicated openly and fairly to all involved.

❖ **Firm** - It is also important to be firm when enforcing the rules. Being firm doesn't mean being harsh or punitive; rather, it means standing by the established rules and maintaining consistent expectations.

❖ **Consistent** - When rules are applied consistently, boys can predict the consequences of their actions, leading to a better understanding of cause and effect. Consistency also fosters a sense of stability and predictability, providing boys with a secure foundation upon which they can explore and learn. Many parents misstep on this point. Inconsistent reinforcement of rules can lead to repeated testing. Keep your rules to a minimum and then be sure to be consistent in their application.

### #2: Love

❖ Even if the behaviour itself is unacceptable, your son needs to know he is loved, unconditionally, always. Knowing that he is loved regardless of his actions provides him with a strong emotional foundation and helps build a secure attachment with you.

❖ Even during moments of misbehavior, it's essential to separate the action from the child. By addressing the behavior while reinforcing your love for your son, you can help him understand that his worth and identity are not solely defined by his actions. This approach fosters a sense of self-worth and self-esteem, enabling him to develop resilience and cope with difficult emotions.

❖ Show that you empathize with his struggles. Empathy involves understanding and acknowledging his feelings, even if you might not agree with his actions. When boys feel that their parents truly comprehend their emotions, they are more likely to open up and share their thoughts and concerns. This open communication strengthens the parent-child bond and helps boys feel heard and understood.

❖ Empathy also plays a crucial role in guiding your son through challenging situations. Instead of immediately punishing or criticizing him, take the time to listen and empathize with his perspective. Acknowledge his feelings and let him know that his emotions are valid, even if his behavior needs improvement. By doing so, you create an environment where he feels safe to express himself honestly without fear of judgment.

### #3: Understanding

❖ Your son needs to know that you understand the emotion behind his behaviour, even when he doesn't. He may not always have the words to articulate his emotions, especially during moments of frustration, anger, or sadness.

❖ Be a patient listener and encourage open communication. Listen to your son and try not to judge what you hear. Let him share his thoughts and feelings at his own pace, and avoid interrupting or dismissing his concerns.

❖ Provide gentle reminders of expectations for behaviour. As your son explores the world, he might push boundaries or forget certain rules. Remind him of appropriate behaviors in a kind and constructive manner, emphasizing that you believe in his ability to make positive choices.

## #4: Safe space

❖ Your son needs to have a space where he knows he can be vulnerable and share all of his emotions. Societal expectations and traditional gender roles might pressure boys to suppress certain feelings, leading to emotional bottling up.

❖ Encourage open communication and let him know you are always there to listen, no matter what he wants to share. Be attentive and actively engage in conversations with him, showing genuine interest in his thoughts and feelings.

## #5: Connection

❖ Punishing only weakens your connection, and takes away his sense of safety and belonging. Connection is the foundation of trust, understanding, and mutual respect. When your son feels connected to you, he is more receptive to guidance and learning. He understands there are consequences for his actions without the external force of punishment.

❖ Relationship based discipline builds integrity and increases emotional intelligence. Instead of resorting to punishment, opt for guidance and support that will help your son understand the consequences of his actions, and be involved in finding solutions to conflicts or misbehavior.

# Your Son's Emotional Bank

*I recall inviting the parent of a second grader to discuss her son's behaviour at school. His teacher had attempted to communicate with the parents previously but there had been very little improvement, prompting her to seek my support as principal.*

*Dave had been sent to my office a few times and although he was showing some improvement, I knew we needed a stronger connection with the home in to truly have an impact.*

*Dave's mom said she was at the end of her rope! Dave was constantly getting in trouble at home, too, and all she seemed to be doing was punishing him for misbehavour. It was wearing down everyone.*

*When I asked when was the last time they did something fun together, she struggled to recall a recent occasion.*

*Something needed to change.*

There will be times in your parenting life where you feel like you are caught in a whirlwind, and your interactions with your son revolve mostly around discipline and punishment. It is an easy cycle to fall into. Remembering the 7 to 1 rule of the Emotional Bank can help you and your son get on better footing in your relationship and deepen your connection rather than weakening it.

Dr. Stephen Covey, author of *The 7 Habits of Highly Effective Families*, talks about this in connection with the relationship between individuals. The deposits in this bank are those things that build trust and strengthen the relationship, and the withdrawals decrease that trust. The balance in the Emotional Bank account determines the quality of communication and problem-solving between two people. When communication with your child seems to be filled with negative emotions and tension it may be time to focus on making more deposits.

Deposits consist of honesty, kindness, unconditional love, patience, and other essential virtues that create a reserve in his bank account. We can make deposits when we:

❖ apologize when we make a mistake
❖ deeply listen when they are talking to us

- ❖ spend time with our child and really be present
- ❖ keep our promises
- ❖ laugh with them
- ❖ notice what they are doing
- ❖ are patient

As parents, we can sometimes, unintentionally, make withdrawals from our son's account. But, when we understand and are aware of what deposits and withdrawals look like, we can focus on making more deposits and building a deeper connection with our child. Common ways we make withdrawals include:

- ❖ nagging, yelling, and criticizing
- ❖ being sarcastic in our communication
- ❖ talking negatively about them or their behaviour
- ❖ being dismissive when they are trying to talk to you
- ❖ checking your phone when they are talking to you

Being mindful of our choices and actions can help us create strong connections. When we actively show our children love, support, and understanding, we are filling up their Emotional Bank. When their account has more deposits, our communication is more open and honest and our relationship is deeper.

*A rule of thumb is this:
for every 1 withdrawal that we
make, we then work on having 7
deposits.*

# Connection Through Action

We all know that our little boys seem to have an abundance of energy. That energy is often viewed in a negative light but understanding the 'why' might change our perspectives and let us see the beauty in it.

Research in the fields of neuroscience and education shows that boys' brains really do work better when their bodies are moving. This highlights the positive impact of physical activity on cognitive function as well as academic performance.

Movement triggers the release of neurotransmitters like dopamine, which enhances focus and motivation.

Executive functions, which involve skills like problem-solving, decision-making, and self-control, are positively influenced by physical activity. Regular movement helps strengthen these cognitive abilities allowing boys to better manage their behaviors and emotions.

And perhaps for everyone, physical activity is linked to improved mood and emotional regulation. Boys who are encouraged and allowed to move and be active tend to exhibit fewer behavioral issues.

Parents can utilize this knowledge to connect deeper with their sons. Although each child is unique, physical movement can support challenging areas of behaviour.

The overly sensitive boy may have a lack of self-regulation; is worried about something; feels fear that he cannot articulate. Try taking a walk in the woods or by the seaside when he is struggling.

The angry boy may not be able to recognize his emotions; may not have developed appropriate coping strategies; may be worried or embarrassed about something he cannot verbalize. Take his favorite ball and go to the park and play.

The shy boy may be unable to verbalize big worries and fears; is cautious of anything new and wants to understand it fully; needs to develop strategies to handle things that are new. Go camping together and experience the unpredictability of nature.

The over-excited boy may be unable to detect their inner 'engine'; needs help to regulate his excitement; lacks calming strategies for building anticipation. Before addressing misbehavior try going on a family bike ride, or a run together first. Then talk.

## *Screens*

Considerations around the use of screens in young children:

We are raising children in a digital age, which is both exciting and a bit overwhelming. The rule book keeps changing as more is researched and discovered. Parents need to look at the pros and cons, learn what they can, and make decisions to the best of their ability. If you are concerned that screen time is negatively impacting your child, take steps to move in a different direction.

**On the Pros side:**

❖ High-quality educational apps, games, and videos can provide interactive and engaging ways for children to learn new concepts, skills, and even language.

❖ Well-designed educational programs can help children grasp complex concepts, foster creativity, and provide exposure to diverse topics and cultures.

❖ Interactive activities on screens, such as puzzles and problem-solving games, can stimulate cognitive development, critical thinking, and reasoning skills.

❖ Screens can present information through visual and auditory formats, catering to different learning styles and enhancing comprehension.

❖ Virtual tours and interactive simulations allow children to explore different places, historical events, and scientific concepts that might otherwise be inaccessible.

❖ Co-viewing and co-playing can create bonding opportunities, where parents and children engage in screen-based activities together.

❖ Some digital platforms offer opportunities for creative expression through drawing, music composition, and storytelling.

**On the Cons side:**

❖ Delayed Social Skills: Excessive screen time can reduce face-to-face interactions, hindering the development of essential social skills such as communication, empathy, and understanding nonverbal cues.

❖ Limited Physical Activity: Increased screen time often leads to sedentary behavior, reducing opportunities for physical activity and healthy movement, which is crucial for their overall health and development.

❖ Disrupted Sleep Patterns: Prolonged screen exposure, especially before bedtime, can disrupt sleep patterns by interfering with the production of melatonin, a hormone that regulates sleep.

❖ Reduced Language Development: Excessive screen use might replace time that could be spent engaging in language-rich activities, such as conversations and reading, potentially impacting language acquisition and vocabulary development.

❖ Attention Issues: Constant exposure to fast-paced visuals and rapid screen changes can contribute to attention-related issues in children, making it difficult for them to focus on tasks that require sustained attention.

❖ Unhealthy Eating Habits: Extended screen time can lead to mindless snacking and a lack of awareness about eating habits, potentially contributing to unhealthy eating patterns.

❖ Developmental Delays: Over reliance on screens might lead to delays in certain developmental milestones, as screen time might replace opportunities for active learning through hands-on exploration.

❖ Risk of Negative Content: Children might inadvertently be exposed to inappropriate or harmful content online, impacting their emotional well-being and understanding of the world around them.

❖ Reduced Imagination and Creativity: Excessive screen use can limit opportunities for imaginative play, which is essential for fostering creativity, problem-solving skills, and cognitive development.

❖ Strained Family Relationships: Excessive screen time can lead to reduced quality time spent with family and caregivers, affecting the development of secure attachments and close relationships.

❖ Addictive Behavior: Excessive screen exposure, particularly to engaging games or social media, can lead to addictive behaviors and difficulties in regulating screen time.

❖ It's important to strike a balance between screen time and other activities that support children's physical, cognitive, emotional, and social development. Parents are responsible for setting healthy screen time limits, curating content, and providing diverse opportunities for learning and growth beyond screens.

# *Boys In Focus: Raising Awareness*

## Shame

It's usually during these years that boys first show how strongly they feel about any situation that causes shame or embarrassment. Shame is about feeling such a fear of humiliation and embarrassment that little boys would prefer to be alone with their pain than to show anybody their vulnerability. So, when you put everything together, little boys just starting out in school have a lot stacked against them. They don't communicate quite the same or as quickly as girls. They don't hear quite the same. The teachers are usually female. They have an increased need to be physical and the possibilities of that are greatly reduced. It's no wonder that some boys respond with misbehavior.

Boys will often shut down when they're having their big feelings and this is when Timed Silence is necessary. When you tell a boy to use his words it's difficult for him because the areas of the brain that connect emotions and language are not as developed as girls. A boy might also be challenged to know which words to use.

Help him develop a 'feelings vocabulary' by talking about your own emotions or emotions that other children are experiencing; asking questions to help him define his emotions such as, 'You seem really upset. What are you feeling right now?' Help him connect physical reactions to the underlying emotions. 'I see your face is getting red. Are you feeling angry?' Use I statements. 'I feel --- when you ---'. Use books and movies to teach and recognize emotions and emotional vocabulary. Play games like 'Name That Feeling' by reading faces in real situations.

## Looking Deeper at Shame

Boys will try to avoid shame at all costs. Shame is that feeling of wanting to crawl under a rock and never come out. You feel worthless, like no one likes you and you just aren't good enough. You expect to be judged or rejected, and you feel powerless. Often when little boys are shamed, adults are trying to motivate them, but the actual result is that the boy feels he isn't capable and he may either start to shut down, or get very angry. When a boy is shamed, he feels bad about himself and starts to believe he cannot change.

Boys who experience shame often feel completely unheard and misunderstood. These feelings often create a lot of anger and hurt. If these continue to be pushed down deeper as time passes, a boy, or man, may end up not being able to feel a lot of positive emotions and even when he does, it is more difficult to express them.

Whereas girls don't like to feel shame, for boys the experience is greatly amplified. Boys will do absolutely anything to avoid being shamed and when they are, it is devastating.

For example:  The Grade 2 teacher might tell your son to move his desk out into the hallway since he can't stay focused and sitting during class time. To your son, that feeling of being embarrassed and ashamed in front of the entire class, as well as anyone who passes him while he is outside in the hall, is the worst possible pain he can feel. He feels hurt, misunderstood and not good enough. He starts to feel he can't do anything right at school so might as well give up. He knows he will get in trouble whatever he does.  Nobody will ever be his friend again. He is too stupid.

This scene or something similar, unfortunately, is not uncommon. But even when things are challenging at school, you have the opportunity to create a home environment in which he feels loved and valued, and where all of his emotions are acknowledged. This space is often referred to as a Shame Free Zone. Your son needs a safe haven at home where he understands that he is more than enough, just as he is. This understanding will enable him to navigate challenging situations outside, knowing that he has a safe space where the pressures of the outside world can fade away.

Despite our well-meaning intentions, we might unknowingly form habits that elicit feelings of shame in our sons. By recognizing this, we can proactively work towards improving our communication strategies.

## Ways you might be shaming your child:

❖ Not Letting a Child Do Things for Themselves

Instead of building up his self-esteem you are reinforcing he is helpless. It often takes more time to let children do things, but if they CAN then they should be allowed to. When you do it for them you are actually taking their power away - shaming them.

❖ Judging Your Child's Choice

When you say things like, 'What were you thinking?' or 'I can't believe you just did that,'" the message that your son takes is that he is not good enough to make good choices; that he is bad.

❖ Telling Them Not to Cry
This reinforces that he can't trust his own emotions and that crying is an unacceptable behaviour. He is not behaving like a good boy.

❖ Setting Expectations Too High
This creates more feelings of failure and not being competent or capable to do anything.

❖ Time Out or Public Discipline
When a boy is publicly shamed it amplifies the pain. The whole world sees that he is a failure, no good, unworthy.

❖ Using a Harsh Tone or Laughing at Your Child
This kind of undermining shaming sends the message that the boy isn't even worth being spoken to respectfully. It must mean the boy is a failure as a human.

❖ Telling Them They are Not a Big Boy or Girl
This labeling shames a child into internalizing that how they really are is not ok. They are not ok. They are unworthy, a failure.

Why is this so important? What are the negative consequences when our child often experiences shame?

## The Effects of Shame

* ❖ Shaming children may lead to compliance, but not for the right reasons.

Children who are shamed might develop a distorted view of themselves as unworthy or flawed.

They may become compliant merely to avoid trouble and focus on a negative self-image (they are bad) rather than reflecting on their actions.

They may struggle to make internal connections that foster doing the right thing or act with compassion and empathy.

* ❖ Shaming can result in children resisting parental limits and feeling ashamed of their own impulses, hindering the development of empathy.

Instead of looking outward and understanding other's experiences, shame turns their attention inward, making it harder for them to show empathy.

* ❖ When children internalize feelings of worthlessness, they might adopt a mindset of having nothing to lose.

This can lead them to seek power over those they perceive more vulnerable, similar to the toxic cycle of bullying.

❖ They learn that shaming someone is an option to model.

They have learned that it is acceptable to shame others when they make mistakes, leading to critical, judgmental, and righteous behaviors as a way to handle problems.

Shaming models dysfunctional ways to deal with problems

❖ It encourages lies and secrecy in an environment that is not safe to do otherwise.

Children learn that this is how they can protect themselves. They will avoid truth at all costs if it means they protect themselves from being vulnerable to being shamed.

❖ Shaming can disconnect behaviour from the child's sense of self.

If a child owns up to his behaviour that would confirm the negative self-image they have adopted. Keeping it disconnected, children deny any ownership of negative actions and their potential impact on others.

With an understanding of the significant influence that shaming can have on boys and an awareness of how we might inadvertently contribute to this, the next step is to explore how we can effectively nurture the emotional development of our growing boys.

# Beyond Shame: Strategies for Empowering Boys

The outside world your boy lives in often encourages him to repress his emotions, so it is extremely important that in the safety of his home he feels safe to express his feelings and thoughts.

Aspects to consider:

❖ Continue to look for the emotion behind the behaviour.

Search to find the emotion that is triggering the behaviour. We need to remember that what we see (the behaviour) is often not what is really going on (the emotion). When we look for the pain our child is holding, rather than react to the misbehavior, there is a better chance that we will deal with the situation with compassion rather than the possibility of trying to shame our child into compliance.

❖ Expand and increase their emotional literacy.

The better equipped our boys are with emotional literacy, the better they will be able to express their real emotion rather than resorting to misbehavior to mask it.

❖ They are always watching you. Be the person they need to see.

Our children learn more from our actions than they do from our words. Make sure you aren't shaming others in the house, or using shaming talk about characters on TV or in the news.

❖ Believe the best of your son. He will become what you see.

Just as shaming can have grave consequences for your son, so can positive talk have a powerful impact on how your son views himself. When you see and acknowledge his good characteristics, he will come to believe them, because he trusts your judgment.

❖ Resist the urge to label & compare.

Be mindful that children often become what we see them to be and call them. If you want your son to be his best, don't label him negatively or compare him to another where he looks weak or lacking.

❖ Be your son's champion. Stand up for him.

Advocate openly for your son. Don't let people tell him to behave according to the Boys Code rules. Let him see you stand up for him and for all boys' right to own their emotional world.

The connection between shame and self-esteem is evident. Emphasizing ways to expand your child's positive self-perception will significantly impact their life experiences.

## The Role of Self-Esteem in Raising Your Son

Self-esteem is our beliefs and feelings about who we are and how much we value ourselves. It is shaped by our own thoughts, relationships and experiences.

Self-esteem creates a feeling of well-being and paves the way for the chance of positive relationships with others. It helps to protect ourselves from mental distress and despondency and has us be more open to learning and feedback.

How we view ourselves greatly impacts how we lead our life.

Understanding self-esteem and its significance in raising your son is important in shaping his overall well-being, confidence, and ability to handle life's challenges.

**Some things that steal self-esteem from our child are:**

❖ Focusing on his weaknesses.

*'Joey, you are so lazy! That's why you are getting so fat. Get outside and run around and turn off that computer.' 'Yes, Joey is a smart boy but he is just plain lazy. That's why his report card isn't as good as it could be.'*

Constantly highlighting and dwelling on your child's weaknesses can undermine their self-worth. Fostering a balanced perspective that acknowledges their strengths and areas of improvement can help them develop a healthier self-image.

❖ Giving him everything.
*'I know everyone has that new phone and I don't want you to feel left out, so we will get one for you this weekend.' 'Those shoes are really expensive. Are you sure you really need those ones? If you feel like you just have to have them, then those are the ones we will get.'*

While it's natural to want to provide for our child, giving them everything they want without teaching them the value of earning or appreciating what they have might lead to entitlement. Encouraging them to work for and appreciate their possessions can help build a stronger sense of accomplishment and self-worth.

- ❖ Being afraid to set limits.

  *'I've told you I don't want you going down to the creek alone with those boys. I don't think it's safe. But, I understand how important it is to you to be with those boys, so maybe we can make an exception just this time.'*

  Avoiding settling limits and boundaries out of fear of upsetting your child can inadvertently make them feel unguided or unsupported. Appropriate limits give them a sense of structure and help them understand acceptable behaviour, which contributes positively to their self-esteem.

- ❖ Showing frustration and making discipline look hard on a regular basis.

  *'You are giving me such a headache. Now I have to cancel my plans because of what you have just done. When am I going to be able to trust you to do what you say you will do?'*

  If discipline is consistently accompanied by frustration or negativity, it can create an impression that the child is inherently difficult. Strive to approach discipline with patience and understanding, emphasizing learning from mistakes rather than creating a perception of contact conflict.

❖ Getting pulled into power struggles regularly.

> *'We've been through this before. Why can't you just do as you are told?'*

Frequent power struggles can make a child feel as if their opinions and desires are constantly at odds with authority figures. Minimizing power struggles through effective communication and conflict resolution can help maintain a healthier dynamic and foster their self-esteem.

❖ Rescuing frequently.

> *'I am so glad that I was there when Bobby did that to you. That could have been quite a serious situation, but luckily I could step in and tell him to stop.'*

Constantly stepping in to solve problems or rescue your child from challenges might inadvertently convey the message that you don't believe they can handle things on their own. Allowing them to navigate certain difficulties independently, with your guidance, can boost their self-confidence.

❖ Using lectures and repeated warnings often.

> *'I've told you a hundred times what would happen if you keep behaving like that! Do I*

*need to remind you of what happened last time you got in a fight?'*

Overusing lectures and repeated warning might create a sense of constant criticism or being talked down to. Instead, opt for open conversations that involve active listening, where they feel heard and understood, to promote a more positive self-perception.

**Some things that boost self-esteem in our child are:**

❖ Focusing on his strengths.
 *'That was such a kind way to help that other little boy solve his problem. Your communication skills are truly impressive.'*

 Acknowledging and highlighting your child's positive attributes, talents, and virtues fosters a sense of accomplishment and self-worth. By recognizing his abilities and efforts, you are strengthening feelings of competence and worth.

❖ Having him work for what he wants.
 *'I understand you want to buy that new game. Maybe you could sell some of your old games at a yard sale to raise some money. Can you think of any other ways to make money?'*

Encouraging your child to earn what they desire cultivates a strong work ethic and a sense of responsibility. When they achieve their goals through effort and determination, they experience the gratification of their hard work paying off. This achievement bolsters their confidence and reinforces the notion that they have the power to influence their outcomes.

❖ Setting limits - expecting him to behave.
*'We've agreed to limit screen time to 30 minutes on weekends. If you struggle with this rule, I'm here to help you by removing the screen. Once we both believe you are ready to try again and can manage your screen time without complaints or anger, we'll revisit this arrangement.'*

Establishing clear boundaries and expectations helps your child understand acceptable behaviour and societal norms. When they meet these expectations, they experience a sense of competence and belonging, allowing them to navigate the world more confidently.

❖ Guiding him to own and solve the problems/conflicts he creates.
*'It looks like Frankie is very upset with you. Can you explain to me what happened?'*
*'OK. I think I understand. How are you*

*going to fix the problem and help Frankie
to feel better?'*

Allowing your son to take ownership of the problems or conflicts he contributes to empowers him to develop problem-solving skills. Encourage him to reflect on his actions, consider alternatives, and take responsibility for finding solutions. This approach not only builds his self-confidence but also equips him with essential life skills to tackle challenges independently.

❖ Avoiding lectures and repeated warnings. When we use too many words, too often, our boys tune out. Simple, concise conversations will create an environment for guidance and support.
*'Frank is hurt He needs your help.'*

When we consider our own children, can we identify the indicators of a well-grounded, robust self-esteem? Are we aware that diminished self-esteem can manifest in various disguises? The more we can recognize these signals within our own child, the better position we will occupy to be able to support them.

# Common Traits of children with Low Self-Esteem

❖ Resistant to trying new things.
   *'No, I don't want to go bowling with the class. I'm no good at it.'*

Children with low self-esteem often exhibit hesitancy or reluctance to engage in new activities or challenges. They may fear failure or judgment, which can hinder their exploration and growth. This resistance stems from a lack of confidence in their abilities.

❖ Speak negatively about themselves.
   *'I'm just stupid anyway. Nobody likes me.'*

Negative self-talk is a common trait. Children who frequently use self-deprecating language or express doubt about their capabilities are likely struggling with their self-worth.

❖ Low tolerance for frustration (giving up easily/waiting for someone else to take over).
   *'I can't do this! Just do it for me, OK?'*

This child displays impatience and gives up easily when faced with difficulties. They might lack the perseverance to overcome obstacles and may prefer to pass the responsibility to someone else. This behaviour usually stems from a lack of self-assurance.

❖ Overly critical and easily disappointed in themselves.
*' I thought I'd get 100% on that test. I guess I didn't study hard enough. That was really stupid of me.'*

These children tend to be overly self-critical and set unrealistically high standards for themselves. They might be easily discouraged or disappointed when they perceive their performance as falling short of their expectations.

## Common Traits of children with High Self-Esteem

❖ Tend to enjoy interacting with others. Children with high self-esteem typically exhibit ease and enjoyment in social interactions. They feel confident in their ability to engage with peers and form positive relationships.

❖ When challenges arise, they can work toward finding solutions and voice discontent without belittling themselves or others, displaying emotional maturity and self-confidence. These children tend to approach challenges with a problem-solving mindset.

❖ They know their strengths and recognize and accept the areas they need to work on. They accept these aspects of themselves without dwelling on them negatively. This self-awareness contributes to a balanced self-perception.

❖ A sense of optimism prevails. These children tend to approach life with a positive outlook, believing in their ability to handle challenges and achieve success. This optimism arises from a strong sense of self-efficacy.

## The Faces of Low Self-Esteem, and How to Recognize Them.

❖ The Imposter - acts happy and successful, but is really terrified of failure. Needs continuous successes to maintain the mask of positive self-esteem, which may lead to problems with perfectionism, procrastination, competition, and burn-out.

❖ The Rebel - acts like the opinions or good will of others don't matter. Lives with constant anger about not feeling good enough.

❖ The Victim - acts helpless and unable to cope with the world and waits for someone to come to the rescue. Uses self-pity or indifference as a shield against fear of taking responsibility for changing his or her life. Problems with unassertiveness, underachievement, and excessive reliance on others in relationships.

Parents hold significant influence over their children's self-esteem. By being vigilant and well-informed, you can ensure the most favorable outcomes for your children's emotional well-being.

## What can parents do?

❖ Provide balanced feedback. Offer your child well-rounded feedback by acknowledging their attempts at new or challenging endeavors. Even when their efforts don't yield success, express support for their dedication. Ask if they gave their best and if they enjoyed the experience, emphasizing that value isn't solely tied to being the best or winning. This strategy works well with school report cards. Focus on the effort or 'soft skills' that are reported on and emphasize how much those traits are valued.

❖ Delegate appropriate household chores to your son. This emphasizes he is a valuable part of the family and his contributions are important. Start this early and adjust it as he becomes able to take on more responsibility.

❖ Provide many opportunities for problem-solving. Encourage them to try new things and celebrate their bravery and persistence. Riding a bicycle for the first time involves tackling various challenges. Problem-solving is a life skill worth honing. When our son would make a request that I disagreed with, I would explain the logic behind my stance. I also said I could be flexible if he could present a compelling case for his stance. He needed to be able to overcome the problems I foresaw. This worked really well in the teenage years!

❖ Give extra hugs at the end of a school day, building up his Emotional Bank, which may have had some withdrawals during the day.

❖ Coach your child through challenging situations. Role model effective approaches both in actions and communication.

❖ Show interest in their interests. Be curious and get involved. You will learn a lot about your son by understanding what appeals to them.

❖ Praise your child, but do it wisely, and don't overpraise. Focus on praising the effort involved. Praise is external, talks about the doer and not the deed. It sets love up as conditional and often compares to others. Encouragement focuses on the deed rather than the doer, is honest and specific, and can build on internal motivation. Children who get too much of the wrong kind of praise are less likely to take risks, are highly sensitive to failure, and are more likely to give up when faced with a challenge.

❖ Focus on your child's strengths and support developing them.

❖ Talk about mistakes as being opportunities. Share your own mistakes and how you coped.

**Rule of thumb:**
Anything your child **can** do,
he **should** do.
It might take longer, and it might be
messier, but it goes a long way in
encouraging and empowering your son's
sense of self competency.

## *Communication*

As our little boy continues to grow and develop, communication becomes an increasingly powerful tool to understand and connect with him. While he is expressing himself more independently, you might begin noticing your son facing some challenges in articulating his feelings and emotions, and that his communication style differs from yours.

It's important to recognize that many boys require more time to respond verbally to questions or share their emotions. We can provide our son with the space he needs by offering some wait time, allowing him to gather his thoughts, calm his feelings, and open up when he feels ready. The amount of time your son needs will depend on a variety of factors:

❖ Age: Younger children may need less time, while older children might need more time to process complex emotions or situations.

❖ Severity of the Issue: The more significant or traumatic the experience or misbehavior, the longer the processing time may be required.

❖ Individual Personality: Some individuals are naturally more introverted or reflective and may need more time to process their emotions.

Patience and understanding are key in creating an environment where your boy feels comfortable expressing himself.

By making communication the heart of our interactions with our boys, we empower them to develop emotional intelligence, navigate challenges, and build profound connections. Creating open channels of communication allows them to express their thoughts and emotions freely, fostering a sense of trust and openness. Simple everyday moments like car rides, park visits, or bedtime routines can become opportunities for meaningful conversations. As we become more attuned to our son's communication preferences, we can initiate discussions that help him process his feelings in a non-judgmental and supportive environment. Introducing books and videos that address similar topics to what he is facing in his world, can also facilitate these conversations and provide valuable insights into his emotional world.

During this stage, our little boys continue to expand their vocabulary and communication skills, especially as they acquire reading abilities. Encouraging and supporting a love for reading will benefit them as they make sense of the world and articulate their emotions. Engaging in activities like home scavenger hunts, leaving thoughtful messages in their lunch boxes, and reading books that spark meaningful conversations can help nurture their literacy and communication development. By fostering a positive and engaging reading environment, we can enhance our son's ability to express himself confidently and effectively, paving the way for better communication in the future.

## Nature or Nurture?

What is behind the differences in how males and females communicate?

Some research suggests that gender differences play a role in shaping communication patterns between males and females. These differences encompass various aspects, including verbal and nonverbal communication, emotional expression, and interaction styles. Such disparities may stem from a combination of biological, neurological, and societal factors.

Exploring communication differences between males and females often results in opposing views on whether these differences are ingrained genetically, woven into their

DNA, or if their communication skills are shaped by the environment and upbringing they experience. Expanding this thought, if certain struggles boys face are a result of how we are raising them, then it logically follows that modifying our approach to communication could potentially mitigate or lessen some of these challenges.

## Nature

There is some evidence that gender differences contribute to variations in how males and females communicate.

❖ The male brain appears to receive more neurological 'rewards' for independent behaviour. This inclination can lead to a preference for self-directed actions and solitary problem-solving, possibly influencing communication patterns that emphasize autonomy and self-sufficiency.

❖ The male brain tends to function optimally in situations involving coordinated actions and teamwork. This tendency may explain why males tend to excel in activities that require synchronized efforts and collaborative strategies, fostering communication styles that prioritize group cohesion and joint efforts.

❖ Males typically exhibit more connections from the front to the back of the brain. This heightened connectivity could contribute to their keen physical perception and decisiveness. It might underpin their ability to swiftly make and execute decisions, influencing communication patterns that lean towards clear and action-oriented expression.

❖ Boys tend to outperform girls, in general, in tasks related to physical spatial processing, motor skills, and sensory-motor speed and reactions. This physical aptitude can influence communication dynamics, potentially leading to an emphasis on action -oriented language and hands-on engagement.

❖ Males often demonstrate superior hand-eye coordination and spatial tracking abilities compared to females. These skills can shape communication patterns, favoring precise gestures, and providing a foundation for nonverbal communication that compliments their physical capabilities.

❖ It is noted that boys' hearing abilities may be less effective when contrasted with girls. This distinction can influence auditory communication.

❖ The corpus callosum, the connective tissue that links the brain's hemispheres, tends to be larger in girls compared to boys. This structural difference holds significance in terms of communication and cognitive functions. Girls benefit from enhanced connectivity between the brain's hemispheres, enabling them to engage in more efficient and seamless communication between different cognitive processes.

❖ Many girls exhibit advanced social cognition skills such as understanding social dynamics, interpreting nonverbal cues, and empathizing with others. They often possess strong memory capacity, facilitating the storage and retrieval of intricate social interactions. This heightened social awareness often extends to an acute sensitivity to emotions. Girls frequently perceive emotions as valuable cues for building bridges of connection with those around them. This innate ability contributes to their adeptness at forging and maintaining interpersonal relationships.

❖ The female brain appears to be predisposed to receiving heightened neurological rewards when engaging in actions that foster social harmony and collaboration. This phenomenon can be attributed to the presence of higher levels of oxytocin in girls compared to boys. Often referred to as the bonding hormone, oxytocin plays a pivotal role in promoting human connections and nurturing social interactions. This inherent neurological tendency propels girls towards actions that strengthen social bonds and cooperation.

❖ In terms of physiology, girls are biologically predisposed with enhanced natural abilities for forming and maintaining connections with others. This can contribute to their propensity for empathy, strong interpersonal relationships, and a greater focus on emotional connection.

## Nurture

There is some evidence that communication dynamics between males and females can be influenced by gender biases, evident from early childhood interactions.

❖ The influence of gender biases starts right from birth, with societal norms perpetuating stereotypes. For instance, advising little girls to 'be careful' while praising boys for similar efforts can create self-fulfilling prophecies. This encourages girls to prioritize caution and boys to emphasize risk-taking, contributing to differing communication styles as they grow.

❖ A study revealed that mothers tend to interact more with infant and toddler girls, while boys respond equally to parental engagement.

❖ Other research indicates that fathers converse openly about sad emotions with daughters, while utilizing achievement-oriented language for sons, such as 'proud,' 'win,' and 'top.'

❖ Dads also engage more in singing with girls, while both parents allocate less time to reading and storytelling with boys, which are empathy-enhancing activities.

In essence, the intricate interplay between communication patterns in males and females is significantly shaped by gender biases, starting early in life. These biases often perpetuate stereotypes that impact how children perceive themselves and others. Research demonstrates how caregivers inadvertently treat boys and girls differently, influencing their communication styles and emotional development. While structural brain differences might not account for the variations, these patterns underscore the importance of fostering unbiased and supportive environments for both genders to communicate, express emotions, and build crucial social skills.

Some neuroscientists, like Dr. Lise Eliot (author of '*Pink Brain, Blue Brain'*), believe that although there are some innate brain differences between boys and girls, those differences at birth seem to be very subtle. More apparent is research that shows social norms act as self-fulfilling prophecies, steering children into predefined gender roles and expectations. While the influence of nature and nurture remains intertwined, societal constructs play a significant role in shaping our understanding of gender distinctions.

## How can parents support their son's communication skills?

We play a critical role in nurturing and enhancing our sons' communication abilities. Through conscious efforts, we can effectively address potential challenges that may arise.

From the very beginning we can create an environment that is rich in emotional literacy - through conversations, modeling, games, books, stories, and more. The avenues for cultivating emotional understanding are limitless.

From the outset, we can explain and exemplify how emotions often underlie behaviors, even though we don't consciously realize it. Something as simple as acknowledging how a lack of sleep can lead to reduced patience can help him connect actions with emotions in real-life situations.

We can point out instances where societal gender biases might discourage some boys or men from expressing vulnerable emotions. Reassuring them that your home is a safe space where all emotions are welcome can foster an environment of open expression.

Our focus on developing these skills will support more developed conversational skills that will help to keep connections and communications deeper.

In conversations with our boys, it's important to remember that not everyone perceives situations in the same way. Even when both parties witness the same event, there's no assurance that their interpretations will be identical. Consider a scenario where a boy is at one end of a number laid flat on the ground, and a parent is at the opposite end. To the boy, it appears as a 6, while to the parent, it looks like a 9. These differing perceptions arise from your distinct vantage points. If your son strongly believes he's correct in a situation, and even if you recognize he's mistaken, prioritize maintaining your connection with him rather than insisting on proving your viewpoint.

What will change the entire dynamics in challenging and emotional dialogue, is adopting a real sense of **EMPATHY.**

❖ Get in touch with what might be going on for your child without getting absorbed / flooded / overwhelmed by their feelings. Keep yourself grounded. You are the adult. Remember that misbehavior is a signal for help; something in his inner world is not right.

❖ Be attentive and curious. When you listen and watch, you will become very aware of how your son is feeling. You might not know why initially, but you will be able to connect.

❖ Whenever possible take an appropriate empathetic / compassionate stance. When your son feels your love, even when he knows you are not pleased with the behaviour involved, he will be more apt to be able to communicate with you.

❖ Express empathy: Non-verbal (hug, touch, soft eye contact,). Verbal (I'm sorry honey, you must be in pain. You look so distressed.)

When you can empathize with the situation for your son, you will have the opportunity to support him and deepen your connection.

I am reminded of a situation that took place years ago during my time at school. A young boy was in the principal's office, anxiously waiting for his father's arrival. It was clear that the boy had committed some misbehavior that necessitated his father to be summoned. I happened to be passing by just as the father and son were coming out of the office. The boy looked very disheartened. In a very touching moment, the father gave his son a hug, saying he was sorry that he had made the wrong choices. He told his son they would discuss the consequences when he returned from school. As he turned to leave he said, 'Love you.' I have never forgotten that.

What are some ways to open up the lines of communication?

❖ Active listening. While this might seem obvious, we often struggle to fully engage when our child talks due to our busy lives. But, when we claim to be listening but don't fully commit, our child senses it - they know we are not fully present. Especially in challenging moments, a more effective approach could involve momentarily setting everything aside to focus truly on understanding our child. If that isn't feasible immediately, schedule a dedicated time, perhaps during bedtime, bath time, or car rides - instances when distractions are minimal. By giving our undivided attention, we send a message that their thoughts and feelings genuinely matter.

❖ Sometimes we simply talk too much and it really can be an overload for our boys. Rather than going on and on about something, try to respond briefly. 'Oh, I see.' 'Hmm'. By speaking less, you create space for him to share more.

❖ Our boys really benefit from our supporting their emotional vocabulary. They may know the feelings but not the words that go with it. Incorporate phrases like, "Oh, that must have been a shock!" or "Looks like you're feeling anxious." This natural approach enhances their emotional language toolkit.

❖ Use a touch of magic by responding to your child's requests with something like, "I wish I had a magic power to… (find your toy)" This communicates your willingness while acknowledging the limitation, fostering a sense of collaboration and teamwork.

Creating open lines of communication requires intention and commitment. By incorporating these approaches into your interactions, you nurture an environment where your child feels heard, valued, and encouraged to share their thoughts and feelings.

## *Considerations About Boys*

## Conversations about Gender Stereotyping & The Boy Code

As our boys venture out of the nest, they may encounter a world that expects them to conform to certain gender stereotypes. It's essential for us as parents to be aware of these societal expectations and their potential impact on our sons' development. How can we best help them adapt to societal expectations and still keep their brave hearts intact?

*Jack comes home from Kindergarten singing, "Girls are weak. Chuck them in the creek." How you react will send him certain messages about what it means to be a boy and a girl.*

A great starting point is engaging in candid and honest conversations about gender roles and the Boy Code with our sons. They may feel pressured to fit into specific molds, even if those expectations don't align with their true interests or feelings. By engaging in open discussions, we can help them recognize and challenge these stereotypes. Reassure them that their gender does not define their abilities or limit their potential. Encourage them to embrace their passions and pursue activities they genuinely enjoy, regardless of traditional gender associations.

As parents, it's important to educate ourselves about the complexities of gender stereotyping. The more we understand, the better equipped we'll be to share valuable insights with our sons. Providing them with information and context can empower them to navigate the complexities of societal expectations with confidence and authenticity. By having these conversations, we can empower our sons to challenge stereotypes and embrace their individuality.

## *Top Tips for Raising Your Boy*

These years signify a crucial phase in your little boy's development, as he begins to evolve into the person he will become. He's brimming with optimism, joy, and boundless energy, making his presence truly vibrant. His insatiable curiosity fuels extensive exploration, and his imagination thrives. With the luxury of time, each day becomes a canvas for his creativity, leading to inventive games and heartwarming discoveries. During this period, he seeks your guidance and encouragement as he embarks on fresh journeys. It's a time of wonder, resilience, and significant growth, shaping the remarkable individual he's becoming.

It is also during this phase, that boys often adopt masks to conform and conceal their true emotions. Societal expectations may not readily embrace their vulnerability, potentially causing a decline in optimism, confidence, and confusion. Creating a secure haven at home where he can freely express himself becomes crucial in protecting his emotional world.

To support him, spend quality time together, making him feel cherished and understood, countering societal pressures. Prioritize physical activity to boost his brain function and strengthen your bond through shared movement and activities. Your home can serve as a refuge from external challenges, nurturing his emotional well-being and maintaining a strong connection between you both.

Here are some key steps to consider:

❖ Honor the Need for Timed Silence: After an upsetting experience, respect his need for some quiet time to process his emotions.

❖ Counter the Effects of Shame: Be vigilant in recognizing and addressing any feelings of shame your son may experience.

❖ Acknowledge School Challenges; Recognize the challenges he faces when adapting to school and prioritize physical activity when he's not in school.

❖ Emphasize Boy-Friendly Learning; Help him understand that there's nothing wrong with him; sometimes schools are still catching up to making education more boy-friendly.

❖ Promote Positive Friendships: This can help balance the challenges he may encounter in daily school life.

❖ Reiterate His Worth: Take time to ensure he knows that life is good, and he is deeply loved.

To recap, let's revisit some guidance for parents as they navigate the developmental stage spanning from 4 to 8 years old.

**Encourage Physical Activity**: Boys are often more active and energetic at this age. Providing opportunities for outdoor play, sports, and physical activities helps them release energy and promotes healthy physical development.

**Explore Interests:** Support their interests and hobbies, regardless of gender stereotypes. Whether it's arts, sports, or science, let them pursue their passions without limitations.

**Promote Emotional Expression:** Create a safe and open environment where your son feels comfortable expressing his emotions. Encourage him to talk about his feelings and teach him to recognize and label emotions in himself and others.

**Foster Positive Communication**: Engage in active listening and meaningful conversations with your son. Show genuine interest in his thoughts and experiences to strengthen your connection and build his communication skills.

**Set Clear Boundaries**: Establish consistent and age-appropriate rules and boundaries. Boys thrive when they know what is expected of them and the consequences of their actions.

**Model Respectful Behavior:** Teach your son to treat others with kindness and respect. Model positive behavior in your interactions with family members, friends, and others.

**Encourage Problem-Solving**: Guide your son in resolving conflicts and finding solutions to challenges. Teach him effective communication and negotiation skills to handle disagreements.

**Support Creativity:** Boys at this age are often curious and imaginative. Provide opportunities for creative play, exploration, and artistic expression to nurture their creativity.

**Provide Structure:** Establish daily routines that provide a sense of stability and predictability. A consistent schedule helps boys feel secure and reduces anxiety.

**Read and Explore**: Engage in reading together to stimulate language development and expand vocabulary. Explore a variety of books and topics to ignite his curiosity and love for learning.

**Celebrate Achievements**: Acknowledge and celebrate your son's achievements, both big and small. Praise his efforts and successes to boost his self-esteem and motivation.

**Promote Independence**: Encourage your son to take on age-appropriate responsibilities and tasks. Building independence fosters confidence and a sense of competence.

**Provide Positive Male Role Models**: Surround your son with positive male role models who embody qualities you want him to develop, such as empathy, communication, and integrity.

**Limit Screen Time**: While technology can be educational, set limits on screen time to ensure a balanced and healthy lifestyle that includes physical activity, social interaction, and other enriching experiences.

**Celebrate Diversity**: Teach your son about different cultures, perspectives, and backgrounds. Encourage inclusivity and acceptance of others' differences.

**Show Unconditional Love**: Above all, shower your son with unconditional love and support. Let him know that your love is unwavering, regardless of his successes or challenges.

# *Summary*

Your son's world is getting bigger, and sometimes confusing and frustrating. Your understanding and support are crucial in keeping his self-esteem intact.

Your son still needs a great deal of physical activity that may not be a big part of school days and require another outlet. Providing him with additional opportunities for physical expression can significantly contribute to his overall well-being and emotional balance.

Boys begin to understand the concept of conformity, which can introduce a new set of challenges. School expectations may appear to be more aligned with the developmental progress of girls, which can sometimes create a disparity in the way boys experience the educational environment and experience.

Look for the emotions behind misbehaviors - it is not just what you are seeing. By understanding the emotions behind the behaviour, you can offer more effective guidance and support.

Replacing discipline with guidance and care can yield remarkable results with dealing with your son's challenges. Recognizing a boy's unique pattern of communication after a challenging experience and understanding the need for Timed Silence can create a safe space for him to process his thoughts and feelings.

## *The Top 3 Questions Parents Ask*

*Question #1: My little guy took some time to adjust to kindergarten but he was doing OK by the end of the year. Now he has just started Grade 1 and he is totally out of control. We get daily messages from school about how badly he is behaving and at home we seem either to be in some kind of a battle or he is having a complete meltdown. What the heck is going on?*

This is an all too common complaint of parents of boys. There are several factors in play.

Firstly, look at the academic demands of a first grader today. Several decades ago, Grade 1 was where children first were introduced to formal schooling, and the curriculum was focused on foundational skills and knowledge that laid the groundwork for further education. Letter recognition and basic phonetics along with basic mathematical understanding formed the core of the academic demand. In Grade 1 children were learning how to socially be together in a positive and constructive manner.

Now look at Grade 1 today. The Language Arts curriculum requires children to acquire phonemic awareness, decoding skills, comprehension and vocabulary. Students are expected to read and understand a variety of texts. They will form sentences, paragraphs, and short narratives with a focus on grammar, punctuation, and spelling. The Math includes counting, place value, addition, subtraction and basic mathematical operations. Children will learn to recognize shapes, understand measurements, time and money. They also will be introduced to basic data collection and interpretation. Is there any need to go on?

There is a greater academic focus, and a more demanding curriculum for Grade 1 students today. While this may work well for some, there is an increase in young boys who are facing challenges to meet expectations. Often the result is behavioral concerns.

There is some evidence that suggests boys might benefit from having a delayed start to formal schooling, by a year or two. This delay would ensure a better developmental readiness for boys. Boys often mature slightly slower than girls, both physically and neurologically, so the benefits of a delayed start for boys would help put them both on more even footing.

Your 6-year-old son struggles to sit still for extended periods, needs to move his body and use his hands to explore and create. In Grade

1 there are more restrictions, more expectations, and less play. Boys often begin to face self-doubt as they are not the kind of students their female classmates are. As their self-esteem takes a blow, they may try and find other ways to build up their confidence - often not with desired behavior. It can be a tough place for a little boy!

Even if the school environment doesn't change there are things you can do as a parent that can have a significant impact on your son. Here are a few ideas:

❖ Keep in mind the Emotional Bank. If you know your son is facing a number of withdrawals daily at school, work on creating more deposits at home.

❖ Understanding his need for physical activity, see if you can squeeze in some exercise before school and again afterwards. 20 minutes running around the park or playing catch in the backyard is a great way to start off his day.

❖ Share your understanding of how your son best learns and how you are supporting that at home. Share information about gender considerations that impact your son's emotional world. Collaborate with the school as much as possible.

❖ Have open and honest conversations about your son's experiences, and challenges, at school. Listen with curiosity and empathy and share gender information with him as well.

*Question #2: Teddy just turned 7 but he is still such a mama's boy! He doesn't have many of those male traits like being tough and independent and I am worried he is going to start to get bullied because he is so soft. How do I toughen him up so that he fits into society better?*

The Boy Code tells us how our boys should behave and feel, but if we understand and are aware of how this negatively impacts our boys, we can make changes. If you can focus on Teddy's self-esteem and show him unconditional love, then he will understand that he is OK just as he is, and will not have to wear a variety of masks to pretend to be someone he is not. His connection to his mother is a beautiful thing - keep that connection strong.

*Question #3: I am really concerned that my 8-year-old is addicted to screens. We had more limitations when he was younger, but we have let him have more control on his screen time as he got older. It is at a point where he would rather play with his 'online friends' with some game than play a real game with real people. We tried to cut back on his usage a few months ago and it was so horrible for the entire family that we caved and gave him full access again. We are at a loss as to what to do!*

As difficult as it might be, you are the adult in this equation, and it is never too late to change things. Letting things slide may work in the short term but the outlook for a positive long-term outcome is grim. Try these strategies, brace for a period of turmoil and chaos, and then commit to moving forward.

❖ First, have an open and honest discussion. Present some scientific facts and share why you are so concerned. In a non-accusatory way, explain how you see his current usage is negatively impacting him and the family. Own up to your own mistakes in not creating better boundaries earlier.

❖ Talk together about establishing clear and consistent limits for usage. Compromise where you can but make it clear that boundaries are set in order to improve the quality of life for everyone.

❖ Create screen-free zones in your home or particular times of the day that will be screen-free.

❖ Explore some alternative activities that are new and exciting. Join a team or group that does an activity your son loves. You want to create more of a balance with physical movement and social connection.

❖ Lead by example. Your actions are far greater than your words, so be mindful of the message you are sending with your own screen time.

# *Final Thoughts*

## Raising a boy to become a remarkable man.

In the final stages of writing, I shared what I had done so far with my son. He asked me a question. "Mom, when someone is finished reading this, will they be able to raise their sons better?" Without hesitation I could answer, "Absolutely!"

I envision a parent who is raising a boy, perhaps struggling at times with that, to be searching for answers and be led to this book. It will fall into the hands of those who need to read it, and who are ready to tap into the knowledge shared.

Their whole world will be shaken up when they become aware of how deeply entrenched gender bias is. They will never see males the same. They will never witness the media without picking up on the subtle messages being sent out about how boys are supposed to feel and behave. They will begin to question everything. That is when the magic begins to happen. Eyes wide open.

The parent who sits and reads these words when they should be sleeping, or doing any one of the million mundane things that occupy most days, who simply cannot stop discovering about the emotional world of their boys, that is the parent this book is meant for. Deep inside you know there is an important message here just waiting for the next page to be turned.

You will read, highlight sections, and write in the sidebars. You know this is what you need to start you on the incredible path to a deep understanding of how to raise your son so that he has the best chance to become a remarkable man.

Once you take the initial deep dive into understanding about gender bias and the complex emotional landscape of boys, your perspective will undergo a profound transformation.

This book started out with a depth and breadth worthy of a university course. There was so much I wanted to share! It was a bit overwhelming for me to write, so in my heart I knew it was too much for a parent in the throes of raising a boy. I reflected on what I really needed when I wore those same shoes. I needed guidance especially in those younger years. All those books I read had good information and added to my growing tool shed, but more and more it didn't feel like they were talking about 'my boy'. Intuitively I knew I was missing something. Once I understood what that was, everything changed. That is why I wrote this book. To help you find the guidance and information that will change everything for you, and your sons.

Nothing, absolutely nothing, will have more of an impact on your son than you. Parents are powerful influencers in their child's world. Even if things don't change in his world fast enough, he will be able to balance his world if he knows you understand and you have a strong and deep connection.

To have that kind of a relationship, you need to understand intimately how the outside world affects your boy's inner emotional world. Boys are treated differently than girls. It is a fact. Much of how or why that happens is unconscious but it still greatly impacts how our children feel about themselves and how they see themselves in the world. Little boys are often conflicted and confused with the dichotomy of this.

They don't understand why adults around them are so protective and sympathetic with the little girls and at the same time they are meant to feel they are supposed to be tough and not need that protection or warm and fuzzy interactions.

They are confused and then angry at how unfair school seems at times. The little girls seem to do everything right and the teachers love them. The boys struggle to stay still and on task and often the apparent cause of a tired teacher's lack of empathy. Little boys start to lose themselves and feel they are just not good enough.

But that little boy, whose parents have fallen into the embrace of this book, is greeted at the end of his school day with love and understanding. His Emotional Bank gradually is replenished. His parents understand the challenges. They are on the same team. He goes to bed that night feeling safe, loved and cherished and ready to start the next day with an open heart and an excitement for life.

As parents, when we can understand deeply about communication and all aspects that either undermine or encourage it, we can understand what it takes to grow and support a relationship with our child that keeps us connected - through the hard times as well as the joyful ones. When we stay curious about our boy's inner world and respect how he best communicates with us, then he will feel safe to share that world, even when he feels most vulnerable. We are his anchor in a sometimes-turbulent world. We can set the groundwork to always be that safe haven.

I believe that each generation of parents does their best to make the world just a little bit better for their children. We are not yet at a place where the world is a fair and equitable place for all.

Consider this anonymous poem:

*For every strong woman, tired of faking weakness, there is a weak man, tired of faking strength.*

*For every woman, tired of faking "foolishness", there is a man tired of having to act as a "model of wisdom"*

*For each woman tired of being labeled as an "emotional female" there is a man who has been denied the right to cry and be sensitive*

*For every sportswoman whose femininity is questioned, there is a man forced to compete in order to give testimony of his virility*

*For every woman tired of being considered a sexual object, there is a man concerned about his sexual performance*

*For every woman who has not had
access to a dignified salary, there is a man
forced to bear the economic responsibility
of another human being.*

*For every woman who ignores the
"secrets of car mechanics" there is a man
who doesn't know how to "boil an egg".*

*For every woman that steps toward her
freedom, there is a man who rediscovers
the road to liberty.*

*The human race is a two-winged bird:
-one wing is female,
-the other is male.
Unless both wings are equally
developed
The human race will not be able to fly*

We are all different; men, women, boys, girls. No two humans are the same. Imagine a world where our differences are acknowledged, respected and valued. Where we live together in a world where we collaborate and support each other rather than compete and undermine.

Maybe we can't change the world this time round. But we can change our own world and the world of our children. Eventually, that will create a two-winged bird that soars.

# What's Next?

Some of you will want to dive deeper into the world of boys.

★ Browse the offerings at Sonhood Coaching and see what calls out to you.

★ Some may want to have access to both knowledge and a supportive group. The Sonhood Society may be for you.

★ And for a few, you will want the direct guidance, support and accountability that is available working directly with me.

You will know what is right for you.

Reach out for what you need.

**YOUR FREE BONUS**
**@sonhoodcoaching.com**

**The 3 Day**
**Challenge for**
**Parents of Boys**
**+ 1 Bonus Day**

Get ready to have
your world rocked

Kathryne Savage Imabayashi

216